"I remember coming out of your two day Toronto seminar just pumped! Using your techniques, I came in to work the very next day and sold a pool, a sauna, and a hot tub to three different individuals!

Your 'words' and knowing 'how' to use them tactfully in order to 'lead' the customer down that all important focused sales path (without them even realizing it) became so evident through your seminar presentation.

The focus you put on 'transference of belief' and how to do that was very powerful to me. What that meant to me was that if I want to be successful in sales long term, I needed to really listen to the client's needs first.

Marco listened to my presentation as if he were my customer and whenever he would see a more effective way of wording something, he would stop me, let me know what might work better and then I would try it. Soon after, I found myself using these new words and selling more because of it. I also found that through personal training sessions with Marco, I was able to tweak my presentation to be more product and people focused.

Marco's guidance has helped me in so many areas of sales and taking care of the customer all of which I am extremely grateful to have ever crossed paths with him. His time and words have helped my everyday job turn into a lifelong career with enthusiasm!"

Rande Zechoval
Oasis Leisure Centre
Wpg. MB.

"Marco's sales techniques and training provided immediate results; sales persons began "closing" twice the number of sales. Sales staff was able to confidently "sell" not only Hot Tubs but any form of merchandise using Marco's approach. Marco maintained a professional manner while at the same time peppered his presentation with humour and passion."

Shirley Moore
Eric's World
BC

"I contacted Mr. Longley to arrange a sales training session in the UK with our sales staff, and without exception, he left them enthused and better able to handle customer's objections and other sales associated issues. His help to me personally and also with our staff, was immeasurable and we found dealing with him an absolute pleasure."

Theo Mantoura
Bromley Hot Tub group
UK

"Marco's excitement and enthusiasm towards the sales process was contagious. His training seminars were always very informative, fun and made the process very enjoyable. Each time we met, he shared his expertise and I couldn't wait to apply it to my own sales transactions with my next customers. Marco made the sales process seem so easy and relaxed. Our sales staff became so comfortable with his suggestions that it became natural to utilize it during every sales transactions with our customers….which then meant more sales closed."

Debbie Goch
Niagara Hot Tubs
Ontario

"You are, without a doubt, one of the best speakers and idea men that I have had the pleasure to know. Your ideas and ingenuity in the sales market are invaluable and infinite. You are a pleasure to work with and we have utilized your ideas with great success."

"Marco's sales knowledge and training skills are excellent. His energy during his two day seminar certainly engaged the audience and ensured our renewed commitment to sell hot tubs.

Marco was always attentive to our needs and was able to represent the right amount of objective perspective that has elevated our sales technique and marketing skills. We appreciated that he listened to our specific concerns and offered solutions, nudging us in the right direction.

It has always a pleasure to deal with Marco and we highly recommend him as a solid addition to any professional sales, marketing and training team."

Julie & Steve Malecki
Hot Tubs Warehouse Direct

"He, by far, exceeded any other sales professional we'd been associated with. Marco provided us with techniques, sales training, advice, guidance and in turn, we were able to increase our sales. He kept in touch and up to date on methods and ideas."

Irene Bruce
Cindy Savitsky
In Hot Water Spas

"Marco's strongest asset is his ability to engage people and he uses this strength in his sales training. Marco designed our dealer sales training programs which were comprehensive, yet easily adaptable from one-on-one training with new sales staff in dealer stores to annual dealer convention group sessions of 100 people or more."

S. W.
Surrey, BC

"I have been involved in the pool and spa business for almost 30 years and have never enjoyed a professional speaker as much as I did when I attended one of Marco's sales seminars. The intensive seminar was educational, engaging, entertaining but most of all…it was fun. I highly recommend Marco's training for anyone that is seriously interested in increasing their profits"

G.W.
Vancouver Island, BC

"It's all about building confidence, following Marco's seminar, I felt increased confidence in myself, my products and my company at an all time high. I applied his materials the first week back on the job and sold a spa and a gazebo with minimal effort coupled with *huge enthusiasm. It was the BEST day in my 20 years in sales, thanks Marco*

Mr. Z.
Edmonton, AB

""When I first started, I studied all the brochures to learn the products but struggled with what to say, when and how to say it. Marco helped me build a road map from the minute the customer walked in all the way through to making the sale."

T.T.
Toronto, Ont

"As an enthusiastic and authentic individual, Marco's confidence and knowledge shone through and he was eager to share his knowledge. Not only was it a fresh and very different approach than any other sales training I'd been to, his animation and interaction made it easy to retain what he taught.

Marco's sales training showed me how to be confident with customers and offer a great experience to each and every person that walked in the door. As a young lady, I lacked confidence in closing. Marco taught me how to overcome objections and ask for the sale every time. The results paid off; this past year we saw a record number of spa sales. If you have the chance to spend some time with Marco Longley, you're in for a treat. I highly recommend him."

Breanne Moncrieff
Paradise Pool & Spa
Trail, BC

The Ultimate

Hot Tub
and
Pool

$ales Book

Discover How To Double Your $ales in 7 Days

Marco Longley

The Ultimate Hot Tub and Pool $ales Book

Discover How To Double Your $ales in 7 Days

Marco Longley

ISBN 978-1-9338-17590

Published by: Profits Publishing
http://profitspublishing.com/

US Address
1300 Boblett Street, Unit A- 218
Blaine WA, 98230
Phone: 866-492-6623
Fax: 250-493-6603

Canadian Address
1265 Charter Hill Drive
Coquitlam, BC, V3E 1P1
Phone: 604-941-3041
Fax: 604-944-7993

Table of Contents

Dedication

I would like to dedicate this book to some very special people in my life, thank you for believing in me when others didn't.

To Anne, my wife, my rock, you rock. You always have an amazing way of making bad days good and good days great. My Mom and Dad, for your unwavering encouragement and belief in me. Little Mitch and little Stacey, you each sit on my shoulders.

Introduction

I have written this book to help you make more money.

I want to acknowledge your courage to learn and congratulate you on your initiative in taking this proactive step to becoming the sales professional you want to be. THANK YOU for investing in yourself and allowing me to be part of your adventure.

After reading this book you will have a better understanding of the fascinating world of selling. You will have all the tools, techniques and strategies to sell more luxury items, whether they be hot tubs, pools, saunas or gazebos. While the book is written and geared directly to successfully selling hot tubs, the concepts are the same for selling anything in your store, be it a hot tub, a pool, a gazebo or a backyard setting. Anything.

I truly believe you will read this book with as much enthusiasm and passion as I have had in its creation. It's been designed to be interactive, with self-quizzes and exercises to provide you with the necessary tools to tailor your presentation to your specific needs, products and services, which will result in more sales. There is a glossary at the back, in the event you are unfamiliar with some of the terminology I have used.

Reading and completing the exercises, and then incorporating these ideas, is just the first step on a journey that should see you better equipped to comfortably handle any sales situation, improve your communication skills both professionally and personally, AND have a lot of FUN along the way. If it is not FUN, you may want to consider a career change.

The book you are reading was written based on years of success-ful selling experience in the pool/hot tub industry, starting in retail sales, resulting in several senior sales management positions with multi-million dollar international companies.

Throughout this book I've referred to the potential client as "Mr. Prospect", which has been the generally accepted term used in sales training manuals for many years. This is not to infer that women never buy hot tubs or pools, but in general, the target market for pools and hot tubs has been male driven. I hope this standard is changing, as I for one, would love to see more women come through the doors to buy a hot tub for their family; recognizing the leisure, health and therapeutic benefits of owning a spa. Likewise, the book often makes reference to sales pro-fessionals being male; fortunately today the percentage of male versus female sales professionals/owners is shifting as we see more women in sales as well as owning their own businesses. I do not want to leave you with the impression that only men can sell spas and pools, as this is certainly not the case. Anyone can sell, and anyone can sell well by understanding the psychol-ogy of the sale. Never discount the power of a woman whether she is a customer , or the sales professional as she is often the controlling factor in the decision making process. I hope that the terminology used does not alienate or offend any individual or group, but that it is understood that it is a term used throughout the book for consistency.

While writing this book, I have deliberately tried to be as "generic" as possible and not focus on any one particular manufacturer or brand, as there are many quality products available. Some sec-tions of the book will relate directly to your particular products and services while some sections may not. Use this book as a guide, a road map if you will, and tailor your presentation to reflect your uniqueness and the uniqueness of your store's varied products. Master your products' unique selling proposition (USP). Whether you are selling hot tubs, pools, gazebos, saunas or any other merchandise you carry just be honest with yourself, the clients you work with and the company you work for. And never forget to have passion and enthusiasm; your prospect will notice both!

Take a little, take a lot from this book. You may be a 20 + year veteran in the industry, or a "newbie" with only a handful of sales under your belt (and not really sure how they happened); every reader can learn new ideas, concepts and techniques to improve their sales. Even the very best sales professionals were once "newbies."

> *"I have been involved in the pool and spa business for almost 30 years and have never enjoyed a professional speaker as much as I did when I attended one of Marco's sales seminars. The intensive seminar was educational, engaging and entertaining, but most of all...it was fun. I highly recommend Marco's training for anyone in the industry that is seriously interested in increasing their profits."*
>
> *G.W.*
> *Vancouver Island, BC*

After actively reading this book and completing the self-quizzes and exercises (no, I can't say that enough!), and applying the concepts, you should see a noticeable increase in your sales. In some cases, dedicated readers have doubled their closing averages.

> *"Marco's sales techniques and training provided immediate results; sales persons began closing twice the number of sales. Sales staff were able to confidently sell not only hot tubs, but also any form of merchandise when using Marco's approach. Marco maintained a professional manner, while at the same time peppered his seminar with humour and passion."*
>
> S. M.
> Prince George, BC

Would doubling your income be something that would interest you? Why? Or worse, why not? Self realization is one thing, self motivation is a completely different matter; what are you prepared to do to increase your sales?

This book has been designed to be read, re-read, dog-eared, highlighted, scribbled in and re-read again on a regular basis. Use it as a reference manual if you find your sales presentation falling flat, if you're in a sales slump or if you feel an area of your presentation needs improvement or fine-tuning.

Wide margins and blank pages have been included for you to write your notes and comments as you explore the concepts and suggestions fitting into your unique style or presentation.

Please take a moment now to answer the six questions below. It will give you a starting point to look back on after you have completed the book and have applied the techniques in the "real" world of selling: your store. Only you will know if you have completed the exercises, as *the results you receive will be in direct proportion to your investment in yourself and career.*

1. Are you satisfied with your current income as it relates to your sales?

2. How serious are you about improving your sales ability?

3. What are your goals in reading this book?

4. Why are those important to you?

5. What would you do with the extra money you earn from increased sales?

6. When is the best time to start earning more money?

_____

_____

_____

_____

_____

_____

_____

_____

I hope you took the time to answer the questions. Nobody is watching, so hopefully you were honest and truthful to yourself. For those that didn't make the effort to answer the questions, ask yourself why. If you truly envision your sales presentation improving and your paycheck increasing, you need to believe in your future successes and put in the necessary work today.

The 80/20 Rule

In my professional experience, the reality is that of all the people who read this book, only **20%** of you will actually make the effort to apply these proven techniques and strategies and see positive change. Only 20% of you will have the courage to break old, ineffective habits and replace them with new and fresh approaches. We all know a commitment to regular exercise will improve our health, longevity and quality of life, but we are creatures of habit and easily fall back into our old and unproductive routines. Change takes effort, work and commitment, coupled with a focus on the future, believing what we do today will affect our lives in the future. You invested in this book for one reason: you want to make positive changes that will result in more sales. Do you really want to see positive change? What are you prepared to do to make it happen?

Sadly, **80%** of readers will make no effort to apply any of these principles, but will put great effort and energy into continuing to focus on excuses. Excuses of how bad the economy is, how competition is killing them, or just fill in the blank with any excuse. They feel justified in their resistance to change and fear of improvement. We ARE in very difficult and challenging business times, so all the more reason to shake up your presentation and make a concentrated effort to learn more to sell more.

Many sales staff (I did not say sales professionals) mistakenly believe it is far easier to complain about how bad business is rather than apply a serious and focused effort to make positive changes resulting in increased sales success. For some, it is easier to skim read this book and disregard the ideas and concepts, without making any effort to try them. They are happier convincing themselves that these ideas won't work in their market.

"Marco, you just don't understand my unique business challenges." I have heard this, or similar comments, many times, from small dealers on Vancouver Island to larger centres like Toronto or Montreal, or even international distributors in Europe. These proven concepts, strategies and techniques work, but only if you apply them.

I once read, "Those that fight hard to keep their excuses get to keep them." I hope that doesn't sound like you.

Will you be in the **rare 20%** group or the **complacent 80%** group? The choice is, and always will be, yours.

Henry Ford, the genius behind the Ford motorcar dynasty, was quoted as saying, "Whether you think you can or whether you think you can't, you're right."

Strong words with an even stronger message if you take it to heart. Take a moment and reflect back to any situation in your life when you said, "I can't," when in fact, "you did."

Virtually every business owner and sales professional, in every market and geographical location, that made the effort to step out of their "comfort" zone and apply these strategies experienced success and saw several incredible results:

- Firstly, the confidence of the sales staff increased dramatically; confidence within themselves, confidence in their store and confidence in their product offering. The old saying, 'If the prospect doesn't buy the messenger, they won't buy the message" holds very true in our business. Have you ever been completely turned off from a product or store because the salesperson didn't appear to have any confidence in themselves or their products?

- Secondly, as sales and confidence increase, sales professionals gain "mental momentum," looking forward to the next prospect and fully expecting a sale.

- Thirdly, you will see an increase in your paycheck and your personal satisfaction in your work.

Would you agree that these are some very nice perks for putting in the effort?

I would like to share with you the comments from one of my dedicated students, Rande Z., after one of my intensive sales seminars.

*"I remember coming out of your two-day Toronto seminar just pumped! Using your techniques, **I came in to work the very next day and sold a pool, a sauna, and a hot tub to three different individuals!** This was the biggest sales day I have ever had.*

Your "words" and knowing "how" to use them tactfully in order to "lead" the customer down that all-important focused sales path (without them even realizing it) became so evident through your sales seminar presentation.

The focus you put on "transference of belief" and how to do that was very powerful to me. What that meant to me was that if I wanted to be successful in sales long term, I needed to really listen to the client's needs first.

*You listened to my presentation as if you were my customer and whenever you would see a more effective way of wording something, you'd stop me, let me know what might work better and then I would try it. Soon after, **I found myself using these new words and selling more because of it**. I also found that through your personal training sessions, I was able to tweak my presentation to be more product- and people-focused.*

Your guidance has helped me in so many areas of sales *and taking care of the customer, all of which make me extremely grateful our paths crossed. Your time and words have helped my everyday job turn into a lifelong career with **enthusiasm**!"*

Rande Z.
Winnipeg, MB

Are you Insane?

There's a famous quote: "The definition of insanity is doing the same thing over and over and expecting a different result each time." My favourite way to say this is: "If you always do what you've always done, you'll always get what you always got".

Does that make sense to you? If you are not ready, willing and committed to make improvements in how you sell, you will continue to get what you always got.

So let me ask you a few questions:

1. Do you want to make more money?

2. Would breaking your old habits and learning new skills and techniques, as painful as you may think that is, help you earn more money?

3. When is a good time to start selling more, have happier customers and earn more money?

Hopefully, you said a resounding "Yes" to the first two questions and a "Today" for the third. I'll say it again: "You will increase your sales in direct proportion to the efforts you are willing to invest in improving your selling skills."

Don't be in the **80%** group that is prepared to settle for average and not willing or committed to make a positive change. If you are still with me, congratulations - you are in that rare **20%** that will see noticeable improvements not only in your sales figures, but also in your professional and personal pride. You owe it to yourself and the company you work with and for to be **your best**.

Many companies have sales reps that are more interested in selling YOU more products than helping **you** sell your products; I am only interested in teaching YOU how to make more money. Did that makes sense? I don't have a hidden agenda, a sales quota to meet or a sales manager telling me what I should or shouldn't do. My goal is simple and singular: to help increase YOUR sales figures and your paycheck. Period.

The Sales "Wheel" and "The Slump"

Each of us has been on the good and the bad side of the wheel; even the best sales pros have bad days or weeks, maybe even months. Don't get discouraged, because it will happen to you as it has happened to me and every other sales professional out there selling every product in every market.

Remember successful selling is a marathon event and not a sprint. Some days you get a "lay down" and can't miss making the sale while other days you think you have completed the best sales presentation of your career, but no sales resulted. Stop. Breathe. In with the good air and out with the bad.

Accepting the good and the bad is a package deal in the profession of sales. If you are consistently missing the sale, it is up to you to figure out why and how to fix it. Change your pitch, presentation or attitude, tone it down or spice it up, but be receptive to making changes and improvements. The best sales professionals in the world are chameleons. Be a chameleon and adjust your presentation to the prospect in front of you. What worked in sales 20 years ago may not work today. Today's prospect is far more educated on your company, your products and your competition than ever before; we can all thank the Internet for that. Instead of getting frustrated with your prospect's due diligence and knowledge, use it to your advantage.

It's All About Attitude and Passion - Just Ask Albert and the Babe

- Babe Ruth is famous for his home run record, but only a few recognize that for many years he also held the record for strikeouts. He hit 714 home runs and struck out 1,330 times in his career (about which he said, "Every strike brings me closer to the next home run.").

- Fired by his newspaper editor, who said he "lacked imagination and had no good ideas," this man went bankrupt several times before he built the largest entertainment company in the world. His name was Walt Disney.

- The story goes that Thomas Edison's teachers said he was

"too stupid to learn anything." He was fired from his first two jobs for being "non-productive." As an inventor, it is reported Edison made 1,000 unsuccessful attempts before successfully inventing the light bulb. When a reporter asked, "How did it feel to fail 1,000 times?" Edison replied, "I didn't fail 1,000 times. The light bulb was an invention with 1,000 steps." Edison held over 1,300 US and foreign patents at the time of his death.

- Albert Einstein did not speak until he was four years old and did not read until he was seven. His parents thought he was "sub-normal," and one of his teachers described him as "mentally slow, unsociable, and adrift forever in foolish dreams." He was expelled from school and was refused admittance to the Zurich Polytechnic School. He did eventually learn to speak and read. Even to do a little math.

- A school dropout and child runaway, this amazing individual used $105 from his first social security check at the age of 65 to pursue a dream and a vision he truly believed in. The world knows him as "Colonel" Sanders, founder of Kentucky Fried Chicken.

Your Perception

Is the proverbial glass half full or half empty? It is up to your perception. A friend of mine is a very successful realtor. At one social gathering, I remember him being asked that question. He replied, "If it isn't Scotch, it doesn't matter."

How is that for a positive attitude? How you see the world and your situation is your perception and may not always be reality. I am never far from a memory of a colleague of mine from years ago, Stevie Huber. Through no fault of his own, Stevie's back was broken in a very serious car accident when his was in his late teens, resulting in him being confined to a wheelchair for the rest of his life. I have very vivid memories of meeting him to grab a coffee. Completely forgetting Stevie's physical limitations, I bitterly complained about the horrible rain and how it had soaked my leather shoes and my dress pants. Stevie, always the optimist, simply smiled and said, "I WISH I could get soaked jumping in puddles."

Boy did that one hit home. I've learned many lessons from Stevie. How many times is the situation truly as bad as we perceive it to be? Imagine a day in your life without the daily gifts we all receive and take completely for granted. What if you lost the gift of sight, mobility or good health? How about the kindness and unconditional love our family and friends give us? Many of us have had the misfortune to attend a funeral and only then create a wish list. "I wish I had called them more." "I wish I had focused on them more than myself."

What if you received the horrible news about the death of a loved one? My wife is a police officer and has had the unimaginable job of waking a sleepy family member, on a cold rainy night, at 3:00 a.m., to inform them of the death of a loved one from a horrific car accident. How would you feel if you were on the receiving end of that notification? Would you wish you had just one more moment to share with them or just one more moment to say, "I love you" one last time? Put the petty bickering and fighting aside and enjoy every moment and the precious time we all have together.

You are probably wondering where I am going with this: the answer is simple. Savour every moment you have, share with the ones you love what they truly mean to you, and live with passion and enthusiasm in your life, not just professionally, but personally as well. There are no dress rehearsals in our lives, just everyday life and living. Life is what happens while you are busy making plans for the future. If you just received news you had a rare cancer and were given three months to live, what would you do differently? Live like you just received that devastating news, as we never know when our time here is up.

The Finest Profession in the World

I believe working in sales is the finest and most fulfilling occupation in the world. When you are at the top of your selling game, YOU can write your own paycheck. How you conduct yourself in selling is entirely up to YOU alone. Only YOU will know if you have truly put the energy, time and work into learning and applying these ideas to be the best you can be. Unfortunately, I cannot be there to see the quality and results of your efforts. I believe YOU can be more successful, but what I believe is not as important as, "Do YOU believe you can be more successful?" Successful selling is not a sprint race, but rather a marathon of always learning to understand your prospect's unique needs and wants. When you put your head on your pillow each night, ask yourself one simple question: "Did I do my very best today?"

Do you have a great successful "selling" story, have creative ideas for overcoming objections or a "Marco, you won't believe the prospect I had today story"? Please share them with me so I can share with others like you. Any submissions published in my next book will receive a complimentary signed copy with my personal THANK YOU for striving to be the very best sales professional you can be and NOT being in the mediocre 80% group.

Enjoy. Learn. Share. Prosper.

Marco Longley

A Brief Review of Closing

In order to properly begin this book, we must first start near the end and work backwards by addressing the one of the most important section of the book, *closing the sale*. Confused? It actually makes perfect sense when you think the *close of the sale* isn't necessarily at the end of your presentation. The close of the sale is just another part of your presentation, as important as all the others; it just gets more recognition because the close of the sale is "the money," "the gravy train," "the payday," "the moola." In order to get to the money, every great sales professional understands that closing the sale doesn't always occur at the end of your presentation. Closing the sale can happen at any time in your sales presentation, if you know what to watch for.

One of my fastest sales of a fully loaded spa was about six minutes. No fluff, no long-winded FAB statements, no ego strokes to the prospect. Six minutes from the time he walked into the store until the time he signed the paperwork. How? I didn't wait until the end of my presentation to close him; I closed him at the greeting. A salesperson at a competitor's store had earlier spent two hours on a presentation, but was not confident in asking for the sale. They provided the prospect with lots of valuable information, the benefits of spa ownership AND a shiny brochure. They even suggested he visit the competition; we were just down the street. They were even kind enough to extend an invitation for him to come back at some future point in time, after shopping around.

Fortunately, my store was the very next shop he walked into; six minutes later the ink on the paperwork was still drying. I did tell him that his was one of my fastest sales. It was only then he shared that he was prepared to buy my competitors spa, but they never asked him. He decided to follow their suggestion so he shopped around. Six minutes. He was primed with knowledge, had a desire to purchase, was educated on spas and ready to purchase. Based on all that background information, I really don't deserve all the credit for the quick sale. All I did was ask which floor model he wanted and if delivery before the weekend would work for him.

Never, ever walk your prospect out of your store without first asking for the sale and NEVER send them to the competitor; it might be me.

By far the most common question I get asked is, **"When is the best time to close a sale?"** This is a great question, if you don't know exactly when the right moment is to close the sale, you will likely try to close too early (you have not built up enough excitement) or too late (the excitement has worn off). Before we get into the nuts and bolts of selling techniques and strategies, let's take a moment to explore some basic, yet very crucial, fundamentals in sales.

The ABCs - Always Be Closing

In sales days long past, the norm was that salespeople used to have a huge presentation with limited interaction or questions of their prospects, which ultimately ended with the question, "Do you want to buy?" Although there have always been incredible sales pros that used this method with great success, today's consumer is far more educated than at any other time in history. Successful selling today requires you to be a professional sales consultant, not just a product peddler. An exchange of questions, ideas and feedback will lead to the right product for that prospect. Are you a product peddler or a skilled sales consultant? A true sales professional doesn't have to wait until the end of their presentation to close the sale; they are always listening for the right moment and will confidently ask for the sale when they feel their prospect is ready to purchase. The terms "close" and "ask for the sale" are synonymous.

So just when is the right time to close the sale?

- In your greeting
- In your credibility statement
- During your discovery
- While giving your presentation
- When creating urgency
- During the close of the sale
- While overcoming objections
- After the sale (in the event you haven't yet closed the sale)

Buying Signals

A buying signal is a verbal OR non-verbal indication that your prospect is visualizing themselves owning your product or using your service. Examples of verbal buying signals are listed below, but also watch for the non-verbal signals such as:

- The prospect walking back to a spa you previously showed them
- The prospect keeping their hands in front of running jets
- A silent distant stare into the bubbling water

I was at a trade show in Northern Alberta, Canada several years ago and met a long-haul ice trucker. For those of you who don't know what that is, these brave souls drive tons of equipment on roads built on frozen lakes, often driving their rigs through the dead of night. I asked him to describe a bad day, as I wasn't familiar with ice trucking. He painted the most amazing and frightening story of blinding snow storms, minus 20 temperatures, creaking, cracking and groaning ice under his truck while he was alone on the icy road at 3:00 a.m. and many miles from anyone or anything - just him in his truck and the creaking, cracking ice beneath him in the dead of night. We talked about how stressed he was by the end of a twelve-hour shift, he described white knuckles, cold sweat and three empty cigarette packs. Not a pretty sight; you could see he was visibly shaken just in describing his day.

Remember ABC? Always Be Closing. Rather than go into a long-winded presentation about our company and the features and benefits of the spa, I walked him to the running tub, asked him to again imagine that white-knuckled, cold and sweaty feeling and THEN I asked him to put his hands in front of the running jets. He did, and then there was silence and his long stare into infinity. Silence. Not a word from him. I bit my tongue several times as I was very tempted to talk and to say something, anything to break the silence. After what seemed like 20 minutes, (which in reality was closer to 60 seconds), he spoke. "I have got to get me one of these!"

This was my other "fastest hot tub sale" and I didn't do anything other than listen to him and turn the jets on at just the right time. Actually, in addition to listening and turning the jets on, I wrote up an order for a fully loaded spa with every option available. Buying signals come in many forms and if you can't recognize them, hear them or connect them to closing, you are missing a HUGE opportunity and losing sales.

Please write five examples of Buying Signals you have heard in your sales career. I'll help you out by giving you the first one to get you started.

"Does it come in a different color?"

_____

_____

_____

_____

How about these:

- "Do you have others in stock?"

- "Do you offer financing?"

- "What's the monthly payment?"

- "How long is that special on for?"

- "This would be perfect!"

ALWAYS follow a strong buying signal with a trial close!

Closing Strategies

The secret to successful selling comes from understanding WHEN to close more than HOW to close. There are two types of closes used in every selling situation, the *trial close* and the more final *closing question*. It is far more important to **open** your presentation than to **close** it; first impressions mean everything. If you are to be seen as a trusted consultant, rather than a "product peddler," you need to uncover and understand the needs and wants of the person in front of you before you start selling.

A *trial close* is any attempt to start closing the sale before the end of your sales presentation. Trial closes are an incredibly underutilized strategy in selling; they are questions that ask for your prospects' opinion and test their readiness to buy (also referred to as 'taking the prospects temperature'). Used properly, they will help you understand when the right time to close the sale is.

In the absence of trial closes, how do you know when it is the right time to ask for the sale? If you are not familiar with using trial closes, initially it *will* be uncomfortable asking your prospects how they feel about your products or what you just presented. This uncomfortable feeling is normal and will pass with practice. You will actually be surprised at how much your prospect will open up and start sharing information with you. Almost everybody likes sharing their opinions and thoughts. You will appear to be genuinely interested in them as you are trying to understand their individual needs. Differentiate yourself from your competition. Remember, your job is to gather as much information as you can to close the sale. Trial closes, when used effectively, will dramatically increase your sales.

A *closing question* asks for a final decision. Understand the difference between a trial close and a final closing question. A final closing question asked too soon can make your prospect feel pressured and they will most likely shut down. The goal of the final close is to get the prospect to say, "Yes" and sign the order.

Trial closes are very powerful; they should be low-key and non-threatening. It is not uncommon for strong sales professionals to use 10 or more trial closes in a single presentation. They should elicit your prospect's opinion about what's been presented and they should be used throughout your presentation.

> *I keep six honest serving-men*
> *(They taught me all I knew);*
> *Their names are What and Why and When*
> *And How and Where and Who.*
> *Rudyard Kipling*

Trial closes often start with words like **how, what, who and would**.

Write down as many trial closes as you can think of. The list is endless and limited only by your imagination. Several examples will follow.

_____

_____

_____

_____

_____

_____

_____

- "How does this sound so far?"
- "When did you first consider purchasing a spa?"
- "What do you like best about this design?"

- "Who do you see using your spa the most?"

- "Does that make sense?"(After explaining a feature or benefit)

- "How close do you feel this comes to meeting your needs?"

- "Would this relieve your aching back?"

- "How would this affect your..."

- "Which of the lifestyle packages is your favourite? Why?"

- "How would you feel if you could reduce your work related stress?

- "What are your feelings about our water sanitation program?"

- "What colors do you prefer?"

- "Who do you see at your first hot tub party?"

Any question that starts with "In your opinion..." is a trial close.

Your prospects' response to your trial close can only be one of the following:

- Strong / Positive

- Lukewarm

- Cold

Positive responses to a trial close are usually a sign you should ask for the sale. The key is to have one or two trial closes committed to memory and ready to use. There is no magic formula – closing is 70% attitude, 20% technique and 10% skill. Prepare yourself, prepare your prospect and do the deed – you owe it to them and to yourself. "ASK FOR THE SALE."

"Well, it certainly sounds like all we have left to do is pick out the right colors. How to do you feel about the white shell?"

"It sounds like this is the one for you and your family. How would you feel if we could deliver this by the weekend?"

Lukewarm responses to a trial close indicate you should continue selling by presenting additional benefits and reasons, tied into their needs.

Cold responses to a trial close mean somewhere your prospect's needs were not understood, discovered or addressed in your presentation.

Any time you get a strong response to a trial close, go for the close!

Setting Up to "Close" the Sale

It is much easier to ask for the sale at the right time, when trial closing questions have been asked throughout the presentation phase of your discussion. You should know the exact moment your prospect is ready to purchase. Trial closes prepare the prospect for the time when you finally ask for the sale.Without trial closing questions you won't have enough information to effectively close a sale.

To Recap Closing Strategies

A trial closing question asks for an opinion while a closing question asks for a final decision.

Notes

_____

_____

_____

_____

_____

_____

_____

_____

_____

The "Why" of the Sale

Before we get started selling, let's first understand the **need** or **want** that motivates your prospect to purchase.

Do you know 10 motivators that lead to your prospect's investing in a spa? After all, if there is no need for a spa purchase, there is no need for what you and I do, which is sell spas.

Be aware of all the reasons that your prospect has when they come in looking to invest in a spa. There is a good chance you can give them additional reasons or suggestions to own and enjoy the spa in ways they never thought of.

"Mr. Prospect, in the winter the average spa is kept between 101 and 104 degrees, but in the summer many hot tub owners never think to drop the temperature to 90 degrees and have a cooling plunge pool in the summer months."

Let's review the **WHY** of a spa purchase.

Health Benefits

Some estimates indicate that 70% of employed North Americans suffer stress-related medical conditions, including insomnia and anxiety. In owning a hot tub, your customers can expect to:

- Relax and reduce their stress levels as water movement relaxes the brain.

- Improve their sleep through 15 minutes of hot water immersion prior to bedtime.

- Enjoy a 'Zen' like setting and relax in a warm and soothing environment.

One of the oldest and safest methods for treating many common ailments is through hydrotherapy. Wear and tear on joints is greatly reduced through gentle exercise in water instead of on land. Many physical benefits result from hot water immersion.

Top 10 Health benefits of spa ownership

1. Relief for arthritis, body aches and stiffness

2. Increased blood flow

3. Deep tissue massage, resulting in relaxed muscles

4. Improved sleep

5. Sweating out toxins

6. Decreased muscle tension

7. Low gravity environment

8. Opening of nasal and bronchial passages for easier breathing

9. Stress relief

10. Decreased pain from headaches

Rehabilitation and Therapy Benefits

Many therapists, trainers and professional sports organizations have used hot water therapy to assist patients in quickly resuming their daily activities. Many of the health benefits of exercise can be received through hot water immersion; as blood pressure is reduced, the heart rate increases. Studies indicate chronic low back pain and knee ailments often benefit from the use of a hot tub.

Family Time

- Quality time with the kids
- Teenagers stay at home
- Creates bonding time
- Similar dynamics to dining together
- All family members enjoying the same activity together
- Relax and enjoy your downtime with your spouse

Social Time

Toss the TV remote away and jump into the spa for some 'after dinner' conversation.
- Party at home with your friends
- Stay closer to home, it's more cost effective and more fun
- After dinner party games can start in the tub
- Chilling out with friends

Outdoor Living

Whether you are beating the winter blues or reveling in summertime fun, hot tubs can be used in any climate year-round. Toss away the cell phone and don't worry about e-mails. Connect with nature as you listen to the sounds of spring and summer or enjoy the cool, crisp air of fall and winter.

The Prestige Factor

Don't forget, luxury items are often purchased for the goal of "keeping up with the Joneses."

Notes

_____

_____

_____

_____

_____

_____

_____

_____

_____

_____

The "How" of the Sale

Now you know the "why" of the sale, let's explore the "how" of the sale. The concepts outlined here can be used to sell any item. The techniques, suggestions and strategies in the book are proven to work. What you get out of this book will be equal to what you put in.

Let me first start by asking, "Why are you reading this book?" Your boss thought it might be a good idea? Your spouse wants you to make more money? Well, I sure hope you answered a resounding "NO" to those questions. I hope you are reading this because you are a sales professional who wants to be at the top of their game. Oh yes, and also make more money along the way…a lot more money!

Do you feel you know everything there is to know about selling spas? If you do, please call me and I will come out and record everything you say and do in a sales pitch. Sales ability evolves every day and you will never know everything. Instead, strive to add one or two new ideas each week to your presentation, more if you want to challenge yourself.

In the unlikely event you are reading this book because you have been told to and you might be thinking, "I really don't have the time or interest to read this," then congratulations, I see why you only sell a handful of spas each year. When I started in sales, many years ago when my clothes were much smaller and I had a few less grey hairs, I learned the art of sales in the school of hard knocks. I lost many sales as I didn't have a clue what I was initially doing or have the luxury of a mentor to suggest areas for improve-ment. I made an effort to study those around me that had the nicer cars and closed the most deals. Years were spent listening and learning from the best salespeople around me, I probably both-ered them with too many questions but never stopped asking. The techniques and strategies I learned from all my years of front line sales helped me sell almost 200 spas in my first year in the hot tub business. That was a good start to my career in spa sales.

You will encounter several exercises and quizzes, no one will know if you complete them or not. Actually, that is not true…YOU will know. I challenge you to challenge yourself and set a goal to double or even triple your spa sales this year.

I have tried my very best to put all my knowledge into this book. No easy task, as you can imagine successful selling is often "thinking on your feet" and not very easy to convert into the written word. I have broken down the "steps of the sale" into easy chap-ters for you to read, learn and look back on as the need arises. I encourage you to read this book several times and make yellow highlights, scribble notes or dog-ear the pages. Do whatever it takes to learn this material.

Are you up for the challenge?

Do you know the origins of the word "sales"? I once read that it comes from the Norwegian word "Selje," which translates literally to "TO SERVE." I am not sure if this is accurate or not, but it really is a great definition. Another definition of sales is the science of learning the desires of a prospect, and then providing that pros-pect with a good product at a fair price to satisfy their desires.

A great sales conversation is constructed of two parts: the con-fidence of the salesperson to ask straightforward questions and the resolution to patiently wait for the prospects' response. While many salespeople may understand the right questions to ask, they do not have the confidence and willpower to allow the prospect to answer them. Instead, they fill the silence with sales fluff, and miss out on the opportunity of discovering what really interests the prospect. Salespeople often cave in to the pressure of silence. Doing all the talking simply shows your prospect you are far more interested in selling them a product than understanding their needs.

You have a head start in the sales game by understanding why your prospect is buying a spa. Here are a few possibilities:

Top 10 reasons to own a hot tub

1. They have a place to put a hot tub!

2. They understand the health benefits of owning a spa.

3. They need or want massage therapy!

4. They have friends or family who already own a hot tub!

5. They believe that they deserve a reward or gift to themselves or their family!

6. Their friends bought a spa and are boasting how great is to own a spa and asking why they don't have one.

7. Their boss or co-worker may have a new spa and the prospect feels that it is a symbol of success.

8. They work hard and feel they owe it to themselves and family.

9. The children keep asking why they don't have one; all their friends have a spa.

10. They like to entertain friends and want a spa to improve their backyard parties.

If you ask a prospect what he likes about a specific hot tub, don't give in after a few moments of silence and start telling the prospect what they should like about the spa. Wait for their answer, and ask them to go on explaining. They may tell you that the size is perfect, or that they love how big the pumps are. Bingo. Now you know what interests them and how you should direct your presentation.

Oftentimes, you'll find your prospects are as uncomfortable with silence as you are. If you can summon enough willpower to await their response, you will find that their words may either close the sale or uncover the real objections they might have.

There is great power in silence, if you know when and how to use it. Your silence shows your prospect that you value their thoughts and concerns. It also shows your prospect that you are confident enough in your product and sales manner that you don't need to resort to sales babble to close the deal.

Remember, the purpose of asking a question is to hear and under-stand the answer. Whatever response you get from your prospect, you'll find that their words were worth the wait.

Notes

_____

_____

_____

_____

_____

_____

_____

_____

_____

_____

The Steps of the Sale

The steps of the sale are the essential building blocks or sequence of events that will move your prospect towards making a buying decision. The product is irrelevant in the sales cycle; it can be hot tubs, swimming pools or million dollar real estate purchases. Understand the different steps of the sale and how to move or transition from one to the next. This is the only way you can be sure all the crucial steps that contribute to the sale have been completed.

The steps to every successful sale should include:

- Greeting

- Establishing credibility

- Discovery

- Product presentation

- Creating urgency

- Closing the sale

- Addressing objections

- Follow-up

Each of these important steps will be addressed in greater detail in later chapters. Transition statements or phrases are small 'bridging' comments that allow you to smoothly move from one step in the sales cycle to the next. They are extremely effective in connecting 'all the dots' of your presentation together. There is a recap of them towards the back of the book for practice. Test yourself and see how well YOU understand and introduce each of these steps in your presentation, not just in your mental checklist, but aloud. It's okay, there's probably no one listening.

Ensure that no matter what mood you are in, your prospect gets a concise and professional sales presentation. If you have been fighting with your spouse, or have just received a speeding ticket, leave those frustrations in your car before you enter your store. Show that you are genuinely interested, professional, and able to address your prospects' varying needs.

Always look for ways to improve your presentation and remember **ABC - Always Be Closing.**

Notes

Greeting Your Prospects

A relaxed greeting to welcome prospects into your showroom will go miles in building a great rapport, which is crucial to earning your prospects' trust and confidence. A potential customer is approaching, your shoes are shined, you've checked your breath and your hair has been neatly coifed. You look like a professional salesperson. NOW WHAT?

You need to make a connection, find common ground and, most importantly, *make a friend*.

- The goal when greeting your prospect is to relax them and begin to build a strong rapport.

- People buy from people they like and trust.

- People buy when they are comfortable.

The Initial Contact

You have heard this before…SMILE! Yup, pretty simple. SMILE, SMILE and SMILE. A smile is contagious and will often be reflected in your prospect.

You must acknowledge the prospects are in your store, but in a very casual, non-threatening manner. In order to get physically close to them, without yelling across your showroom floor, here are several easy methods that always work, in the event you are not comfortable with a casual, yet effective hello.

- Have a cleaning rag in your hand and do a "drive-by." Walk near them with a brief greeting (try, "Thank you for visiting our store.") and wipe down a spa near them. Perhaps you can move an item from one part of your store to the other side.

- Rearrange your plants, spa steps or any other décor feature. Remember how they initially perceive you - as a SALESPERSON! Try to remember how you felt when you were out shopping for an item and you got blindsided by an aggressive salesperson. Many prospects either feel ignored or overwhelmed by salespeople.

- Make a friend and get your prospects to laugh if you can.

Allow them to look around and give them time to get comfortable with your store setting.

Don't Talk Spas

Initially, try to get them to talk about themselves. This is the warm-up part of your presentation; you are building very important rapport with your prospect because you **will** need that rapport later.

Start your dialogue with **anything** other than the products you sell and promote. Ask about an outfit, a child, a piece of clothing, a recent sports game and even the weather. Don't talk about religion or politics. Just be sincere when you ask your questions. Talk with them as if they are already your friend and this may be their second or third visit to your store. Always include every member when you introduce yourself, never leave the kids out, as they can be your best allies or your worst enemies. Do you have a kids play area to keep them entertained in the event they don't want to be dragged around your store? Offer your prospects a coffee or water; it is a very nice goodwill gesture.

Never prejudge your prospect. They may have muddy boots on and a dirty work shirt and look they don't have a dime. I was working with one such prospect and everybody in the store figured I was wasting my time with them. After spending a pleasant 10 minutes warming up this prospect, I moved through my presentation and eventually sold him a spa. As we were doing up the paperwork, I kidded him about tracking mud through the showroom. He apologized and explained his occupation. It turns out he owned one of the largest sod and landscape companies in the country and was easily worth far more than you and I will earn in 10 lifetimes. As he left the store, I watched him get into his brand new Mercedes, muddy boots and all. Never prejudge.

Transition From Your Greeting Into Your Credibility

After an initial warm-up, and your warm-up many go on for 15 or 20 minutes, transition into more of a business focused conversation with, **"What brings you in to our store today?"** (If it rolls off your tongue smoothly, replace "our store" with your actual store name and you have started branding your store name.)

> *"What have you heard about our store?" (Again, use your store name for added branding.)*
>
> *"Mr. Prospect, before we go look at our spas, if you are like most people, you probably have two questions. What spa am I going to buy and from whom am I going to buy it from? Does that sound about right?"*

This is a very important step; you have started to ask questions and proven your professionalism by correctly indentifying their concerns in advance of them bringing them up.

"Let's get started over here." (Direct or lead them to a different area of the showroom, next to your credibility wall made up of pictures of happy spa owners and awards or other forms of your store's recognition.)

You have now taken control and they will follow your lead.

Never say:

- "Hi, can I help you?"

- "Look around and let me know if you have any questions."

- "What do we have to do to make a deal today?"

You should now have very relaxed and attentive prospects that are looking forward to discussing hot tubs with you.

Congratulations, you have started the sales process on the right foot and are now ready to build value as you discuss your credibility.

Notes

_____

_____

_____

_____

_____

_____

_____

_____

_____

_____

Establishing Credibility

The prospect in front of you may genuinely have never heard of your store or the brands you carry, which is why you need to establish that you are a credible business with history. Lead them into the area of your store that physically demonstrates your credibility as a company, which is your credibility wall (posters, awards, letters of recognition, involvement in the community). Do you have a "wall of credibility"? It is an incredibly effective sales tool and very powerful in demonstrating to your prospect that they're dealing with a credible business.

Start the Presentation About Your Store – Not Your Products

Quiz Time

Why should a prospect do business with your store? Give yourself two minutes and write down why the person standing in front of you should do business with you today.

_____

_____

_____

_____

_____

_____

Well, I bet that's one quiz many of you will have struggled with. Only on a rare occasion have I met a business owner or salesperson that gave me a good presentation about why anyone should do business with them. Once you fully understand why your credibility statement is so very important, you will see more success in overcoming objections like "I want to think about it". Only with continued practice will your store credibility statement sound professional.

Earlier I provided you with some very powerful statements for transitioning into discussing your spas and your store. I hope now that you have practiced your "selling your store" pitch and can now share with your prospect many exciting aspects about your store, your business philosophies and exactly why the prospect should feel comfortable in doing business with you. Establishing strong professional credibility will 'go miles' for you in overcoming the objection "I need to think about it" (see the chapter on 'overcoming objections' to better understand why your prospects 'want to think about it' as it relates to store credibility).

How does this sound for a store description?

"Let me tell you a little bit about our store (use the store name) so that you can better understand who we are and what we have to offer. We are a full service company from delivery and water testing, all the way through to factory trained technicians. We look after you before and after your investment with us. This store has been here since ____."

"We were in a similar situation as you many years ago when we decided to start selling hot tubs. Just like you, we did a lot of research as well. Do you know there are almost 100 spa manufacturers in the industry? Each company claims they're the very best with the most unique features. We chose the XYZ Spa Company. And the reason we did,

was their XX years of expertise in spa manufacturing. We couldn't find a better-built spa to sell to our customers - and they are a Canadian company located just outside Vancouver. (Or conversely, if the manufacturer is American, make sure you say so, especially if you are in the US market.) If you went out and talked with our prospects, most would say purchasing their hot tub was one of the best investments they ever made. I often hear comments from new spa owners like, "Why did I wait so long?" and "I've never slept better." ("Bash the Snake's Head" - more on that later in Overcoming Objections.)

"Our customers tell us that their hot tub gives them a higher quality of life and they are confident the quality will be there year after year. Does that sound like the kind of company you would do business with? Yes? Well, we feel exactly the same way."

Credibility Builders

- Memberships in associations, such as BBB, NSPI, etc.
- Photos of happy owners
- Lifestyle images to let your prospect know they're in the right place
- Manufacturers POP materials
- Water test lab is obvious

Credibility Wall

A credibility wall is an absolute must-have in your showroom. It offers credible testimonials from satisfied owners. It's said that a customer's testimonial is one thousand times more effective than what the salesperson says. One of the goals of your presentation, and especially this valuable chapter on credibility, is to not only be credible, but to be unique and different from your competition. Be memorable to your prospect in every aspect of your presentation.

A great credibility wall should contain several items: certificates of professional recognition, photos, awards, testimonials, delivery and/or ownership maps.

Designate a section on one of your main showroom walls in a well-lit, easily accessible area - NOT in the back of your store, away from the showroom, down the a dark corridor, next to the dirty washrooms and garbage cans overflowing with debris, discarded pumps and assorted old plumbing manifolds and bits. Can you tell that description was based on a dealer I visited? You should have a dedicated section of wall space to proudly display your community awards, professional memberships and any other recognizable certificates.

Photo "Wall of Fame"

The main section of your credibility wall will have big and bold pictures of your owner's happy families enjoying the spa they purchased from you. When you receive a picture from a happy owner (more about getting those all important pictures in the "Follow-Up" chapter), have a 3" x 5" card with "What our spa means to us" typed across the top, and below that, the family name, eg., "The Johnson Family." Have your happy owners fill it out in their own handwriting. You are establishing huge credibility here AND silently overcoming objections.

How?

When the 3" X 5" testimonial card is complete (you may even want to write a few of your own cards, based on the positive comments other owners have shared with you), attach it below the picture you have been given. These owner testimonials are pure gold and will tie in with the picture your prospect is looking at, they become terrific silent salespersons.

How?

Imagine if your biggest objection was "I need to think about it." You probably don't have to imagine for long, as this is one of the most common objections we all face. Suppose your satisfied owner had written something like "I can't believe I spent five years thinking about getting a hot tub. It is one of the best things I have ever done for my family, and I have never slept better. I should have done this five years ago." When this short testimonial is placed under the appropriate picture from your owners several amazing things happen.

Firstly, when you get your photographic film developed (Okay, I just dated myself) or more accurately with today's technology, your latest pictures "downloaded", what is the very first thing you look at when reviewing the pictures? If you are like 90% of people, you will look at yourself first, then the others in the picture. Call it ego, call it pride, it really doesn't matter what you call it; let's call it a selling tool. People enjoy seeing pictures of themselves, especially if it is with their families having fun. How proud will your customer be when they see their family up of the **wall of fame**?

What happens if you are in your store alone, or are the only person on the sales floor, with a prospect, when the telephone rings or another person walks in the store? If you tell your prospects to "hang out" or look around until you have the time to speak with them, this is dead and absolutely wasted time. It is not the best way to deal with this situation. It's a lot like being put on hold when you've called someone with call waiting and you're left waiting for them. How powerful would it be to suggest to your prospect the following?

"Mr. Prospect, I must apologize. We're a bit short-staffed this morning. Do you mind if I take a moment to answer

the telephone? Here is something we are very proud of; it's our wall of fame. You will find it very interesting while you are waiting. These are some of our happy hot tub owners. Please take a moment to see if you recognize any of your neighbors or friends."

You have just bought yourself some time and the testimonials on your wall will act as silent salesmen.

I have seen prospects spend 10 minutes or more reading EVERY word and comment on the 'wall of fame' while hoping to see if they recognize anyone. When prompted to continue with the presentation, I have been told, "We are not finished reading yet." What a terrific way to start overcoming objections and planting very positive buying "seeds" in your prospects' mind. Your prospect may even recognize a friend or workmate that owns one of your spas. How would that be for instant credibility?

Create testimonial cards that overcome common objections and the benefit that resulted:

"When we initially looked at your spas, we hoped we might get some more time with our teenagers, as we never knew where they went at night. Now we can't get them and their friends out of the spa. We never worry as we always know where our kids are."

Now if you have teenage kids that are a bit on the wild side, you may not see this as a benefit nor want them in your hot tub every night. All kidding aside regarding the teenagers, a testimonial connected to a photo substantially increases your credibility.

Don't have any pictures from existing owners? Have a free draw for owners that repeatedly return to your store for water testing, explain you are collecting photos for a contest and the winner will receive a prize. Inform them their pictures can be physically brought in or emailed. Give away a small in-store credit as a draw prize.

Maps

What area do you deliver to or send techs out on a service call? Do your prospects understand the value of this service you offer? Have a delivery/customer map riddled with pushpins. If you have a map of your delivery area and dozens, if not hundreds, of push pins, with each pin representing a delivery or a happy customer and it covers two-thirds of the map, what message does that send to your prospect? If you say your store has over 2,000 (your particular numbers) satisfied customers, say it with a map covered with 2,000 pushpins. The push pins don't have to reflect spa owners only, they can represent any customer. If you really want to get creative, make each pushpin color correspond to a different spa model purchased. Make you map big and bold, just make it memorable.

How about a set of delivery photos? Many prospects have no idea what is involved in a delivery. Display a series of photos showing all aspects of delivery from the moment the spa leaves your store until it arrives at the customer's house. Display pictures of your more challenging installations - cranes and helicopters are not that uncommon.

Recognizable Client Names

Do you have a strong relationship with well-known owners or perhaps a customer your prospects would recognize? I consulted for a mid-western pool / spa dealer that had all the city pools and several of the most expensive hotels as their clients for pool maintenance. There was nothing in their store that would indicate this. One of the first things I suggested they did to increase their credibility was to have very large poster-size pictures of the city pools and stunning hotels up on their wall as a testimonial. When the sales staff started their credibility statements, they went something like this:

> *"Mr. Prospect, are you familiar with the ABC hotel (the most expensive hotel in the city), and the DEF hotel (probably the second most expensive hotel in the city)? Well, those hotels, and all the city pools, are our clients for water testing. We are the only pool spa store in the city that looks after them. Why do you think that is?"*

What do you think that did for the store's credibility? I am not suggesting you lie and fake this - just take advantage of the fact your store may have some very recognizable clients with very discerning tastes and budgets that could have spent their money anywhere. They invested their money with you and your store.

By now, you have already taken control, started to overcome objections, and have used a trial close. Can you identify where control was established, how objections were overcome before the prospect brought them up, and where the trial close was?

Notes

_____

_____

_____

_____

_____

_____

_____

Discovery

Understanding the Needs and Wants of Your Prospect

When you truly listen to your prospect, you will understand their needs, wants, concerns and motivators. If you are sincerely interested in fulfilling their needs, the discovery phase will provide you with all the information you need to sell them and how to not to sell them, based entirely on *their* needs.

If you ask the right questions and not only listen, but understand their answers, you should also be able to find out your prospects' **hot buttons** (what keeps them awake at night, so to speak) and what they perceive as being important. From that point, you should be able to determine what will fit their needs based upon what they think is important, not what you think is important.

When you go to a doctor, they ask you questions BEFORE they give a diagnosis, not after. A common saying in the medical profession is "Prescription before diagnosis is malpractice," and the same sentiment is true in sales.

You don't sell someone a product per se. People buy your product when it fulfills their needs or solves their problems.

The strategy behind a great discovery is simple. A true sales professional will **listen** people into buying, rather than **talk** them into buying. It is far easier for people to talk themselves into purchasing, than for you to talk them into purchasing. Think about this: a person goes to the hardware store and purchases an electric drill.

Does he want an electric drill? NO! He wants a HOLE. He buys the drill because it solves his need to create a hole.

- We don't buy gym memberships or ski passes, we buy health and fun

- We don't buy books, we buy knowledge

- We don't buy calendars, we buy efficiency and organization

- We don't buy cars, we buy transportation and prestige

Understand that while you are selling a physical, tangible product, your prospect is purchasing the product for what it will DO for them. Don't put your focus on what your product is; instead focus on WHAT benefits your product will provide. It either needs to fix a problem, satisfy a desire or fill a need. It is up to you to uncover that problem or need. Someone extolling the advantages of a new revolutionary computer mouse to solve carpel tunnel syndrome is wasting their time if their prospect doesn't use a computer. Does that make sense to you?

Write down the name of any ten items you have in your life, and then beside each of them write what it is you actually purchased. I'll get you started:

- A new bed is purchased to provide a good night's sleep of rest and relaxation, thereby increasing productivity and quality of life.

- A microwave is purchased for convenience and time savings.

Your turn:

_____

_____

_____

_____

_____

_____

_____

_____

What are you really selling? Sure, you sell hot tubs and other assorted value items. But really, what you're providing is a solution
to your prospects' problem or to satisfy their need or want. In other
words, what need does your product fulfill?

The Purpose of Your
Discovery Questions

- To get your prospect to do the talking

- To help you understand your prospects' wants and needs

- To help your prospect discover and explain their own wants
  and needs

- To let your prospect know, by your interest and actions,
  you want to help them, not just sell a product

- To help you customize your presentation to better address
  your prospects' dominant buying motives and get the prospects to agree to them

Prospects may ask you a question and you'll immediately proceed
to talk about your product. This one little issue may be why you

are not making more sales. Often it is your product knowledge that keeps getting in the way! It's not that you don't have enough product knowledge – trust me, you probably have plenty. It's that you may not be listening to what your prospect is truly asking you. Salespeople often take questions or statements literally instead of trying to clarify the truth of what it is immediately.

Prospects are not always sure what to ask, especially if they have never owned a hot tub or pool. Have you heard the saying, "You don't know what you don't know"? Oftentimes, prospects will ask questions hoping you will fill in the blanks and help them figure out just what it is they are really asking for.

I recall overhearing a new salesperson telling a prospect about how big their pumps were. The prospect asked if the hot tub would be good for their arthritis, which was a great question (huge hot button). The salesperson said, "Yes," and then continued on explaining the horsepower rating on the pump, right where they left off. They never once referred back the gentleman's pain and discomfort of arthritis and they never sold him a spa. Have you ever done something like that?

Sadly, two things happened that day: a sale was lost and a very nice older man walked out of that store no closer to having his pain and discomfort of arthritis decreased. Take a moment and ask yourself how you would have handled that question. Jot down how you would have addressed it.

_____

_____

_____

_____

_____

_____

_____

How does this reply sound (take your pick of the questions you might ask to build rapport with your prospect)?

> *"Mr. Prospect, it sounds like you are having some major concerns with your arthritis. Do you mind if I ask how it affects you? I understand how you feel. My Mom also has severe osteoarthritis and it really affects her hands and knees, especially in the winter. How does your arthritis affect your average day? How does that make you feel? How are you currently dealing with your discomfort and pain? Do you know of anyone else with arthritis that has benefited from a warm soak and a massage in a hot tub? What would your day be like if your pain was reduced? If I could show you how you might be able to decrease your pain through the use of a hot tub, is that something you would be interested in?"*

Start painting the picture of what the spa will do for them, how they will benefit from the ownership of a hot tub. Use third party stories about owners you have that suffer from the same condition and how their purchase has improved their quality of life (wouldn't it be great if you had their picture and testimonial up on your wall of fame?). Take a moment and actually think about how you would handle this because I can promise you, it will come up again. It may not be a prospect with arthritis; it may be some other painful malady that your prospect will gladly give their hard-earned money to have relieved.

I always said to my prospects, "Twenty years ago, the goal of hot tub owners was the indulgence of frosty beverages and 'naked time' in the spa. Today, the benefits of spa use include relaxation, stress relief and quality family time." This almost always got a great laugh. The list is long so take time to learn it and share with your prospect all the benefits they will receive from spa ownership.

Get Wet

Disappointingly, many spa salespeople have never even wet-tested the spas they sell and, if this is the case, I strongly suggest you wet-test one of your spas today! Get in and try every seat, every jet, every option and feature you sell. How can you speak confidently with authority and enthusiasm on your product if you have never tried it? How can you share with conviction how a certain jet or seat configuration FEELS to you on your back/neck/legs?

If your prospect doesn't buy the messenger, they won't buy the message.

To set yourself apart from your competition you really need to focus your presentation on the needs of your prospect. Many of your competitors will have focused their attention on their product knowledge and will not have really listened to the needs of the prospect. Your prospect will buy from you if you have listened to their unique needs and touched their emotions in the dialogue. People buy with their emotions and justify with logic. It never works the other way round. Sell to your prospects' emotional need to purchase their tub or pool. Well-placed and practiced questions in your discovery are crucial to your success; during your presentation is when all that active listening will really pay off.

People Don't Care How Much You Know Until They Know How Much You Care

Don't get me wrong, exceptional product knowledge is very necessary at the right time, but many salespeople bring it up too soon in their presentation. Your prospect only cares about themselves and fulfilling the needs that they have. Initially, they don't care about you, your products or the company your work for. It is nothing personal, just a fact. Your entire presentation needs to be about your prospect and what your product will do for them and how they will benefit through ownership. Put your product knowledge aside for a moment and focus on your prospects' needs. Remember WIIFM - What's In It For Me? This question will always be in your prospects' mind, don't forget it.

The only way to find out your prospects' needs is with good questions and even greater listening skills. If your prospect asks a specific technical question about your product, then you need to ask yourself why they are asking that question. Think about it for a minute. Most salespeople will immediately attempt to answer the question and go into a product vomit session about the nuts, bolts and widgets of their spa, instead of asking the prospect, "That's a great question. Do you mind if I ask why that is important to you?" They are not having a conversation with you today to buy nuts, bolts and widgets. They are having a conversation with you today for some other reasons, and *it is your job to find out what those reasons are.*

The next time you are getting ready to launch into a long spiel about why your product's specs are better than a competitor's specs, find out why they are asking. It may even give you clues regarding what competitors they have visited.

Riddle Me This

If you could magically read a potential customer's mind, what would it tell you? If you were guaranteed a sale every time because you could read minds, would your sales volume increase leading to bigger paychecks? You bet it would!

How would it make you feel if you could discover the following from reading the prospects mind:

1. What they want

2. Why they want it

3. What options and extras they want

4. When they want it

5. Where they want it

6. What they are willing to pay for it

7. What will motivate them to buy it

8. What it is going to take to get them to purchase that spa from you

9. How they will use it

10. What fears prevent them from moving forward

What could you do with this knowledge?

- Build the road map for your presentation

- Personalize the spa exactly as they want it

- Confirm their delivery date

- Increase their perceived urgency

- Eliminate any and all objections

- Close the sale

- How about receive a huge commission check?

Sounds great! Unfortunately, if you are like me, you probably can't read your prospects' mind, or anyone else's for that matter. If you could read minds, you would probably be relaxing on some warm exotic beach many miles away sipping tropical beverages while coconut scented breezes swirled around you. So what CAN we do in place of reading our prospects' mind? We can ask questions, listen and try to understand their answers.

Rather than **talk** someone into buying a spa, next time why not try **listening** them in to a spa? If I have a prospect in front of me and I don't uncover his sore back or stressful job because I am too busy telling him all the things I think he needs to hear shame on me. I didn't do my job of uncovering their buying motives, their needs and wants and have failed them.

Oftentimes in sales, we are all guilty of "data dumping"- telling the prospect everything we "think" they need to hear about a spa, but never asking them, "Why do you need a spa?" or "What is important to you in owning a spa?" We have all "data dumped" at one time or another. It's a comfort zone we fall into when we are not sure what to say next or where to take the conversation. We often make the mistake of falling back to presenting the features and technical specifications of our products instead of discovering our prospects' needs and motivators.

Can you recall an example of when you "data dumped" on a client with your incredible recall of technical details? Did it help you get the sale? It probably did not help unless you were presenting to an engineer. Early in my sales career, I thought it was very impressive to data dump; unfortunately, it was usually met with a glazed and dazed look. I can guarantee you that the person with the pain of arthritis is far more interested in how your hot tub will ease their discomfort, than knowing what the amperage draw is when pump #2 is engaged.

So how do we get the prospect to tell us their needs? Simply ask great questions and understand the answers. Believe me, this is far easier said than done. Well-placed and phrased questions will result in your prospect feeling their needs and concerns are being addressed. Ever play 20 Questions? Were you closer to guessing the correct answer before or after asking your 20 questions?

Ask open-ended questions. Open-ended questions require your prospect to provide a more detailed answer than just YES or NO. Open-ended questions usually start with How? When? What? Where? The list of questions is long and only limited by your creativity. Role-play with your colleagues and get comfortable asking open-ended questions.

Transition From Credibility to Discovery

After completing the credibility phase of your presentation, you need to smoothly move or transition into your discovery phase. Try this transition statement:

"Mr. Prospect, in order to better understand your plans and ideas, do you mind if I ask you a few questions?"

It really doesn't get much easier than that. You now have your prospects' permission to ask questions throughout your presentation. This will be especially helpful when they throw objections at you; you have permission to ask questions at any time to better understand their concerns. How respectful is that question to your prospect?

Top 10+ Sample Hot Tub Discovery Questions

As long as you have built strong rapport, the type and number of questions you can ask is limitless. In the absence of a strong rapport, you will have a long road ahead of you as your prospect might feel they are being interrogated. Here is my Top 10 list of discovery questions, plus a few thrown in for good measure.

1. "Have you owned a hot tub before?"

2. "What is your reason for wanting a spa?"

3. "What need will the hot tub meet for you?" (Rest, relaxation or therapy)

4. "How long have you been considering a hot tub for your family?"

5. "Where would you place your hot tub?"
   (Have they already picked out a spot?)

6. "How many people will be enjoying your spa?"

7. "What is your experience in using a hot tub?" (Friends, hotels, etc.)

   - "What did you like about the hot tub experience?"

   - "Was there anything you didn't like about that hot tub?"

8. "What hot tubs have you sat in before? (This question helps to uncover if they've visited your competition.) Doesn't that sound better than asking, "What other stores have you been to?"

   - "Was it comfortable?"

   - "What did you like about it?"

   - "What didn't you like about it?"

   - "Why didn't you purchase it?"

   - "How were you treated at that store?"

9. "What seating arrangements do you like - lounger or bench seating?"

10. "Are you doing other renovations or additions to your home?" (Deck, patio, etc.)

11. "What's your time frame for getting into a hot tub?"

12. "Are there any privacy concerns in the placement of your hot tub?"

13. "How familiar are you with the ease of maintenance of our hot tubs?"

Try to probe deeper when you have an answer to a question. These are called "second level" questions. Use their answers to generate more questions. If you were asking about house renovations, take the extra time to ask questions regarding what they are doing even if it doesn't relate to hot tubs, because it relates to them. If they are building a garage, listen, ask questions and learn about what interests them...garages!

Come up with a list of questions of your own that you are comfortable asking. You should arrange this list with your most important questions in the order that will make most sense to you.

_____

_____

_____

_____

_____

_____

_____

_____

Don't Be A Tour Guide

By the end of your discovery, you should know exactly what spa and options you feel will best suit their needs. If you are not sure what spa you need to focus on, ask more questions. If you don't have a direction to go, you will end up being a tour guide and they will be left confused and unsure which spa is the best for them. Have you ever lost a sale because you gave too many choices?

Does this sound familiar:

> *"We just can't decide. We have to go home and think about it."*

When you go to a restaurant, do you ever suffer from indecision because there are too many great choices on the menu? Do you find yourself changing your mind at the last second when you hear your friend order the steak special when you were considering the seafood special? Don't be a tour guide! You are the professional making professional suggestions based on an understanding of their needs.

The more time you spend talking WITH and not TO your prospect will result in them being more relaxed and they will trust your opinion and suggestions. Your prospect also has a time investment with you and realistically probably doesn't want to spend another couple of hours at your competitor's store. If you have understood their needs and given a great presentation in a professional and thoughtful manner, then you're on your way to making the sale.

Transition From Discovery Into Presentation

You now have to transition from your Discovery phase into your Presentation phase. After you have asked as many questions as you feel are necessary to understand their unique needs and wants, you should be able to present the perfect spa. Recap your dialogue with your prospect to prove you have listened to what they said and are sincerely interested in addressing their needs. Show them you are the expert and they will follow your lead.

> *"Well, Mr. Prospect, if I understand you correctly, you are looking for _____ and you need it because_____.*
> *You need seating for_____ people and you already have your electrical set up. (Recap all the details you learned in your Discovery that address your prospects' specific needs).*
> *"Do I have that correct? I think we have the perfect spa for you and your family over here. Please follow me, as there are a few great ideas I would like to show you that would fit your needs perfectly."*

Wow, how do you think your prospect will feel about you and your opinion after you have recapped everything that is important to them? You will have truly separated yourself from your competition and you are well on your way to making the sale.

OR

> *"Well, Mr. Prospect, you have really given me some great information (everyone likes to think they are not only being listened to, but actually heard), which will allow me to make some terrific suggestions. Let's step over here as there are a few things I would like to show you".*

If you have completed a dynamite Discovery, you will have all the tools and information you need to sell your prospect their perfect spa, based on their needs and wants. Take your time in your presentation and include their "hot buttons" while you present your spas and how they will benefit from owning one.

Notes

_____

_____

_____

_____

_____

_____

_____

_____

_____

_____

_____

Spa Presentation

It's Showtime

Your time to shine is during your presentation. By now your prospects should have warmed up to you, credibility of you and your store has been established and your discovery has provided you with all the information that is important to your prospect. You should also have been continuously building a great rapport with your prospect. If not, you may be falling flat on your face, before you even begin your presentation. Here is where all that hard work and effort starts paying back big time. Use all the information you gathered during your warm-up, credibility and discovery to personalize your presentation to your prospect. Wrap it all up with passion and enthusiasm into a bulletproof offering and your prospect can't say no.

The Knee Bone is Connected to the Shin Bone

A logical, easy to follow product presentation is essential for helping your prospect easily absorb the information you are presenting. A well-ordered presentation helps move you and your prospect ever closer to achieving the goal of making the sale and having a happy customer.

BBQs are Evil

Have you ever assembled a BBQ from a kit? If so, you will understand the comparison I am trying to make about using a well-planned, logical and orderly presentation. Having assembled far too many cheap $99 BBQs, I have found the assembly instructions are usually extensive, frustrating, requiring an engineering degree and often impossible to follow, even on a good day. Assembled incorrectly, your BBQ can easily end up looking like a strange "UFO-like" sculpture suitable only for exhibition on the roadside. In the unlikely event the instructions are followed perfectly, you will be grilling burgers and hot dogs before the sun sets, the envy of all your neighbors that were unsuccessful assembling *their* BBQs.

Imagine purchasing a BBQ or receiving one as a gift. You excitedly open the box with anticipation of enjoying frosty beverages and sizzling burgers in an hour or two, only to find a booklet with "388 pages of easy-to-follow instructions." In addition to your "easy-to-follow" instruction guide, there are about 2,000 pieces that all look identical, each needing to go in the right place at the right time and in the right order. Easy, yeah right. (Note to self: next time spend the 40 bucks and have it assembled.) You can pretty well say goodbye to your next three weekends as you attempt to assemble your BBQ so that it looks like the picture on the box that all 2,000 pieces came in. Sound familiar? Every piece, part and section requiring assembly is directly related to your success in having correctly completed all the assembly as it relates to the previous piece, part and successful assembly of the part before it. Did I say that correctly? If you are confused, you are not alone. Welcome to the wonderful world of BBQ assembly.

What all this should mean to you is if the assembly steps aren't followed in a precise and well-ordered fashion, no burgers for you. You might as well order a pizza.

Enough About BBQs

I think you get my point about the challenges associated with assembling a BBQ. A well-ordered and logical product presentation is crucial for several reasons. It reduces the chance of you confusing your prospect by jumping back and forth from feature to credibility, back to warranty and then on to technical specifications and delivery. These are all important topics you need to address, but they must be presented in a manageable, logical order. You need to present your spa features and benefits in an order that is easy for your prospect to absorb and understand. A *planned* presentation provides you with the freedom to go off topic and come right back to where you left off and not miss covering any important information or features you may have forgotten while sidetracked.

Keep in mind, I am NOT advising you to use a *canned* presentation, but following the same structured and logical presentation steps each time will ensure that you don't inadvertently omit crucial benefits and opportunities to move you and your prospect closer to the sale.

Think of the last time you saw a bad presentation of any product. Was it a sloppy, disorganized and confusing presentation that left you wondering what was just said, instead of seeing the value and feeling "I just have to have that product"? I think it goes without saying this is definitely not the most effective way to sell any product, especially a high-ticket item like a hot tub or pool.

I have seen salespeople switch from jet features, to delivery, to warranty, to siding, to credibility, on to cover lifters and then steps, and back again to jet features, all in a single breath. Did that sound confusing to you? Imagine how that sounded to a prospect that knows nothing about our business. We are in the spa and pool business and what we take completely for granted may be absolutely new and potentially overwhelming to your prospect.

Compare that choppy disordered presentation to a professional presentation. Think of watching a pitchman at an exhibition or tradeshow, or even a late night infomercial selling "Super Knives" or "Floor Sweepers." They are experts at their presentation and it shows, as it is always the same pitch! They can draw you in as you watch and want to hear what they have to say. If you study these pitchmen long enough, who knows what might happen. You might learn a thing or two about why a great presentation works or you might just end up owning a new set of steak knives or a miracle broom.

Don't make your presentation difficult for your prospect to understand or worse yet, difficult for them to purchase your product. It is far easier for your prospect to absorb, understand and connect with your information if your information has been presented in a well-organized and logical order.

Have you ever heard the saying "How do you eat an elephant - one bite at a time?" Your presentation should be in bite-size, digestible pieces. If you are talking about your warranty, stick with discussing warranty related topics until you have covered all the bases. If you are a strong closer, don't hesitate to ask your prospect, "Do you have any questions about our warranty program?" or "Is there anything you need to think about regarding our warranty?" Do you see where I am going with this? I am looking for the prospects' commitment that they completely understood what I said. They didn't have to think about it. When it's time to close them, there is nothing they can throw out as an objection like, "I need to think about it," because they have already confirmed they didn't need to think about it. The only objection or concern I expect to hear when I ask for the sale should be price related and dealing with the price is just a matter of the details.

Painting the Picture - Sell the Sizzle, Not the Steak

Imagine a plump lemon, about three inches long, an intensely vivid yellow. It fits snuggly in the palm of your left hand. As you hold the lemon, a light citrus smell meets your nose. Now imagine taking out a three-inch paring knife with a dark walnut handle into your right hand and gently slicing a thick wedge from the top to bottom of the lemon. A small stream of fresh juice squirts from the lemon and stings your eye as you slice deeply into the lemon. Squinting with your right eye, you bring the succulent wedge of lemon to your lips and bite down hard. What do you feel? Are you in the moment of biting the lemon? Can you taste the bitter sourness of the lemon? I painted the picture with written words that your brain assembled into an experience and produced a reaction. Had I just said "Imagine biting a lemon," would you agree it would not have had the same effect or the same intensity? Why was the first example more visceral for you? I **painted the picture** and guided your imagination to put your mind into the scenario of you actually biting the lemon. The key to a successful sales presentation lays in the fact that we purchase items **emotionally**; we need to get into the prospects' head and paint *their* picture using your spoken words and your enthusiasm.

Imagine you were a prospect listening to the following statements for the very first time. Which description sounds more emotive: A or B?

A. *"This tub has two three-horsepower pumps, full-foam insulation, deep seats, and a 4-inch cover."*

OR

B. *"This particular pump and jetting package has enough power to work any painful kink out of your neck, back or legs, or all three at the same time. In addition to the therapeutic massaging action of the jets, you will be able to enjoy your spa even in the coldest winter nights as the extra deep seats provide comfortable deepwater immersion; protecting you from the wind while still providing you with a comfort-*

able soak in hot bubbly water right up to your chin. How would that make you feel on a cold February night after a long day at work? Our full foam insulation ensures your spa will not only be extremely quiet, you will also enjoy the benefits of saving money in operating costs and any potential long-term plumbing repairs. Our heavily insulated cover is a 'no brainer' as it keeps the heat in and the cold out. Our cover locking system provides you and your family with the added security of knowing your spa is securely locked when you are not enjoying the spa."

Both statements have a similar message, yet are completely different. This is an example of selling the sizzle and not the steak. Would you agree the option B **sells** the spa emotionally, as opposed to "technically" or "logically" as in example A? When your prospect begins to imagine themselves using your product, you are heading the right direction and closer to making the sale. Have you ever heard the saying "ownership in the mind"? It is that unique moment when we all "mentally" purchase a product. We imagine ourselves using the product, enjoying the product and sharing it with our family and loved ones (all these are emotional connections) before we have even purchased it.

Create an emotional connection between your prospect and your product and you change how your prospect's decision is made.

Let me say that again.

Create an emotional connection between your prospect and your product and you change how your prospect's decision is made.

Your prospect will fall in love with your product and have a strong desire to own it through an emotional connection that results in them envisioning themselves benefitting from your product over and over again. Any product that will make your prospect happier will become a product of desire. Once the emotional connection between your prospect and your product is made, and the price made truly affordable, will all the other issues become only minor details in completing the sale.

Before a prospect can begin visualizing themselves using your product, they must have the interest and a desire to do so. A unique sales presentation is the most effective way to spark curiosity, interest and engage your prospect. Don't get lazy and fall into the trap of giving them a brochure or a DVD and ask them to come back later. No, I am not kidding about the brochure or DVD, I have seen it one too many times. Shake up your presentation and show your uniqueness, try something different you haven't done or said before in your presentation. Do you know what your competitors are saying and how they are presenting their products? Don't do what your competitors do, because that is exactly what your prospect is expecting you to do. Paint bold pictures with your words that will result in your prospects **owning your spa in their minds**, well in advance of you ever mentioning the price. In an ideal world, you will have injected so much passion, enthusiasm and value into your presentation, your prospect will say, "That's all?" when you finally start talking price. If your prospect believed what you said, loved what they saw and would use it, the only thing missing is to complete the sale. Ask for the sale.

Always paint a picture that they can relate to. If your prospect is a family of five, learn the names of the kids and use them when presenting your spas.

"Mr. Prospect, I imagine you and your wife sitting here and there, while your daughter Anne sits here. Bryan could be using the lounger and little Andrew might sit up here on the steps, as they are a little shallower. How does that sound to you?"

Paint the picture of them using the spa and they will mentally see their spa in use in their own backyard with the entire family enjoying themselves. The moment your prospect can see your product as theirs, the probability of closing your impending sale has greatly increased. Dream the dream with your prospect; their dream is their **hot button**. Keep pressing it and focusing your presentation back to it. Remember they are not buying your product; they are buying what they imagine your product will do for them and their loved ones. The more vividly you paint the picture and present them with a way of owning their dream, the more likely they are to invest their money in you, your products and your store. No connection means no sale.

- Paint vivid mental pictures, use analogies, be memorable, be animated

- Be FUN - enthusiasm and passion sell far more than product knowledge

- Always maintain eye contact

- Speak to all members of the family (I have sold many spas to the young kids, resulting in the kids having to ask mom or dad for the credit card deposit)

- Always ask questions – don't ever assume

- Don't use industry jargon - you risk losing your prospect and the sale

- Don't ever criticize a competitor - point out why you and your products are the better choice

- You will have learned in your discovery what your prospects are like, what they value and what is important to them - now be the superstar and use that information in your spa presentation and sell them

Find the Target

Any marksman will tell you it is harder to hit a moving target than a stationary one, it is harder still to hit a target you can't see. If you don't know what you're shooting at, how do you expect to hit it? Too many salespeople make the mistake of launching into their presentation by telling and demonstrating everything they know about the product (data dumping), without ever knowing what the prospects' needs are first. Conduct a thorough discovery first. Discover what the target actually is. Is the hot tub being purchased for hydrotherapy, quality family time or just entertainment? You need to understand this well in advance of starting your presentation.

Never start selling unless you know what the prospects' wants and needs are. Is this chapter making sense for you? Can you recall examples where you might have data dumped or inadvertently given a less than stellar presentation without knowing the target?

A Round of Golf

I remember walking through a shopping mall and seeing an amazing promotional display with a set of very expensive golf clubs for sale. Now just a little background here, I don't golf. I tried it once and never will again, as I injured my low back many years ago and the twisting component of golf prevents me from enjoying the game. Other sports, yes - golf, never again. I walked up to the display, intrigued by the stunning display and how well designed and eye catching it was. The salesman was all over me, figuratively, in about eight seconds and without even a hello, he launched into his pitch about graphite shafts, titanium heads and leather grips. I didn't say a word and waited for him to ask me a question. No such luck. No questions to or about me were forthcoming.

His product knowledge was impressive, he went on about how the bag was made of the finest materials on the planet and the stitching was first class. Apparently, even the wheels were special, as they had been crafted from some new space age plastic polymer that some chemist had developed just for golf courses. He said they would reduce the rolling resistance of the cart. After what must have been five minutes of him doing all the talking, I finally had to cut him off and say, "I don't golf." His reply will never be forgotten. "Why didn't you tell me you didn't golf, before I went into my presentation?"

Ever had one of those days? I think we all have. Often our enthusiasm and passion for our offering can result in us saying everything we possibly can about our product. It is not for a lack of interest in the prospect; we can all get caught up in our own enthusiasm when we think the prospect is showing any interest. In my case, I liked their display and not their product. Make sure your prospects' interest in your products is for the right reasons (theirs, not yours) and ask questions.

Tradeshows seem to bring out the worst in a salesperson. I can only put it down to a **spin to win** mentality that if the salesperson doesn't close the prospect in two minutes or less, the prospect was never really interested. The tradeshow salesperson often figures it is a numbers game - it's a busy show and there will be a new prospect along in another couple of minutes anyway. I recall seeing a prospect walk up to a salesperson at one such tradeshow, explain they were considering investing in a spa, and watched in horror as the salesperson launched into a canned presentation that their spas were the best and have blah, blah, blah. WRONG, WRONG, WRONG. So where did they go wrong? Think about it for a moment. They started by talking about everything *they thought* the prospect needed to hear. How about starting the conversation with a couple of questions regarding, oh, let's say... EVERYTHING the prospect might ever need or want in a spa, not what *we* think they need to hear.

FAB Statements

Are you familiar with FAB statements (feature, advantage, benefit) as they relate to your presentation? They are an incredibly powerful sales technique that will substantially increase your sales when you master using them successfully.

Your primary focus in selling must be to make it absolutely clear that what you are offering is of value for your prospect. You must explain how your prospect will benefit from ownership. The most effective way to do this is with FAB statements. FAB statements help paint the picture as to why your spa or pool is the most effective means of meeting your prospects' needs. They connect the physical features of your product to the benefit the prospect wishes to receive. The benefit of your product is the reason why your prospect must own it.

Why use FAB Statements?

- They build value in your product and increased value justifies the asking price.
- You control the direction of the discussion and presentation.
- You can better understand your prospects' needs.
- They reduce the chances of you data dumping.
- The prospect will often reveal buying signals.
- You will address their WIIFM.

It doesn't matter if you're the largest, the shiniest or the fastest. How do you know if any of that is important to your prospect? Your prospect will always be thinking **WIIFM - "What's in it for me?"**

Ever Heard of Aesop's Fables?

This old fable is very interesting as it relates directly to WIIFM.

As the fable goes, one day a fox caught his beautiful tail in a trap. In the struggle to free himself from the trap, he lost his tail; all that was left behind was an ugly stump. Initially, the fox was ashamed and embarrassed to show himself to his fellow foxes as foxes pride themselves on their tails.

After months of self imposed seclusion, he finally wanted to put a better face upon his misfortune. He called all the foxes together for a meeting to consider a new proposal. When they had all gathered, the tailless fox proposed that they should all cut off their tails. He explained how inconvenient a tail was when being pursued by enemies and how difficult a bushy tail was to clean after running through the mud and debris. He also shared how often a tail got in the way when wanting to sit down. He failed to see any advantage in having such a useless thing as a tail.

"That is all very well," said one of the wiser older foxes, "but I do not think you would have recommended us to dispose of our tails if you had not happened to lose one yourself."

Your prospect will always be wondering "What's in it for me?"

FAB statements are the most effective and valuable techniques to present your unique features, explain their associated benefits and build value in your product. Effective use of FAB statements will result in increased sales. When you present your products, always remember to translate your features into advantages and then advantages into benefits. The benefit of your product is the reason your prospect will buy from you, as it is the WIIFM that they will remember most. With practice, you will be able to turn that benefit in to a **hook**, a trial close that connects all the dots. Your **hook** gets them to confirm the benefit is important to them.

- **Feature** – actual components of the product (What is it?)

- **Advantage** – what the result of having the feature is (What does it do?)

- **Benefit** – how your prospect will benefit by having the feature (WIIFM?)

- **Hook** – ties the benefit into a trial closing question

It is not uncommon to have many different benefits associated with your unique product features, so adjust your benefit statements to reflect your prospects' specific needs.

Following every feature and/or advantage you mention, transition into what the benefit to your prospect is.

- "What it means to you is..."

- "Providing you with..."

- "What this does for you is..."

- "Which means you will benefit by..."

- "Therefore you will be able to..."

FAB Statement Examples

Built in Steps

"Our 'easy entry' cascading steps (feature) make spa entry and exit much safer and easier (advantage). What this means to you is whether it's your kids, Grandma or yourself, you will have the safest, most stable and secure way to en-

ter and exit your hot tub (benefit). Do you think that safety is important to Grandma? Do you think she would use and enjoy the spa more if she felt safe moving in and out of it (hook)?"

OR

Waterfalls

The feature is waterfalls. The advantage is they create the sound of ocean waves or a babbling brook. The benefit is deep mental relaxation as your mind drifts a thousand miles away to a tropical beach.

"Mr. Prospect, one of our most popular options is our ribbon waterfalls (feature). They mimic the sound of a babbling brook (advantage). What this does is put your mind into an incredibly relaxed, stress-free environment. By simply closing your eyes and listening to the waterfalls, your mind will drift a thousand miles away to a tropical beach with the rolling waves in the background. The massaging jets will relax your muscles, while the waterfalls will relax your mind (benefit). Relaxation is important to you, isn't it (hook)?"

"Mr. Prospect, please close your eyes for just a moment and listen to the sound the waterfalls create. How would that make you feel after one of your long stress-filled 12-hour days?"

Does that FAB statement sound effective in painting the picture? Would that detailed description help your prospect make an emotional connection to your spa as compared to you simply saying, "We have three waterfalls"?

Building Value

In the absence of value, every single selling situation degenerates to one thing...PRICE.

The more value you build into your presentation, the more valuable your product becomes to your prospect.

Features + Advantages + Benefits = Value

The price we ask must be equal to or less than the value that we are able to establish.

Your prospect will pay a higher price for your products and services if they feel the value you built justifies the price. In the absence of value, all that's left to negotiate is the price. A high value will justify a higher asking price; a lack of value will justify a lower price.

To Dive or Not to Dive

My passion, outside of the world of selling, is scuba diving. I use this example because you are probably not very familiar with technical scuba diving and the comparison to spa and pool sales is deliberate. Try to see the parallels between you as a newbie purchasing dive equipment, to a prospect walking into your store to purchase your products. Your prospect may be as unfamiliar with hot tubs and pools as you are with scuba diving equipment. Imagine you just walked into a dive store intent on purchasing dive gear and saw a dive helmet, the MARCO1606, priced at $6,999. You would probably fall down after seeing the exorbitant price being asked. The reason for your "sticker shock" is two-fold. Firstly, you don't have an "anchor price" or anything to compare the asking price to, and secondly, you don't see the value in spending $6,999 for a dive helmet. As the salesperson starts to explain the features,

advantages and benefits of the MARCO1606 dive helmet, you will
see the value of the helmet increase and the price justified.

The following examples would be used after a thorough discovery
phase. At this point, the seasoned sales professional will have
gathered all the information needed and will have moved into their
product presentation phase. Their FAB statements relating to the
features of the MARCO1606 might go something like the examples below. Keep in mind these FAB statements will have been
tailored to the particular needs of the prospect and their individual
diving needs. I have kept the technical and industry jargon to an
absolute minimum. Also remember, the more value the salesperson builds into the product, the more justified he is in asking for
$6,999. In addition to justifying the price, he substantially increas-
es the prospects' desire to move forward with the investment. I
have indicated the individual components, of the FAB statements
in each case.

- "Mr. Scuba Diver, this is an LPN connector unique to our
  helmets (feature). It provides you with instant two-way
  communication with the surface (advantage). You will be
  able to easily talk with your surface crew in real time and
  get instant feedback (benefit). Constant communication
  and guidance from the surface crew is important to you,
  isn't it (hook)?"

- "All our dive helmets have a double neck seal (feature),
  which means the fit between your helmet and dive suit will
  be exact (advantage). The benefit of our double seal is
  less cold water seeping in and around your neck, resulting
  in you being warm and dry (benefit). Would being warm
  and dry when you dive be of interest to you (hook)?"

- "We have a B56 mixing chamber (feature), which will allow
  you to confidently mix different dive gases (advantage),
  resulting in an increased bottom time (benefit). Being able
  to dive for longer time is important to you, isn't it (hook)?"

- "The X7 helmet feature offers a unique bail out system only found on our helmets (feature). It allows you to immediately jettison your gear (advantage) and safely return to the surface in the unlikely event of an 'out of air' situation (benefit). Is safely returning to the surface something you would be interested in doing (hook)?"

- "The MARCO1606 model is the only helmet on the market that has our unique 'gotta go' fittings (feature). These stainless steel fittings allow rapid removal of your helmet and dive suit (advantage). When your morning coffee catches up with you and you 'gotta go', you NEED to get out of your gear quickly and find a bathroom." (Huge benefit, believe me on that one). The hook in this case, should be obvious.

After reading the FAB statements regarding the MARCO1606, and understanding all the features, advantages and, most importantly, the benefits of the helmet, does the price of $6,999 still seem all that outrageous now that you understand the value of the investment?

Dissection of an Effective Spa Presentation

Every showroom is different, from its layout to signage to the individual products you carry in your store. You will find that you probably have a favourite spa or two to work with. As salespeople, we all gravitate to our own favourites for our own individual reasons. Ideally, you should work with a fully loaded running spa to present the very best spa your prospect can own.

To Run or Not to Run

You need to have a fully loaded running spa in your showroom; this is not an option. A running spa is crucial, as there will be many unspoken questions your prospect will have that are only answered if you maintain a pristine running spa. Perhaps they are wondering how loud the spa is when running the spa with all pumps on full. They may be wondering what the spa water feels and smells like or just how quiet that circulation pump really is. Your prospects' unspoken questions may be numerous. Think of it this way, would you purchase a new high-end entertainment system from an electronics store that didn't have any of their equipment pumping out a great soundtrack or an HD movie playing? A fully loaded running spa goes a long way to assist your prospect in easily imagining themselves experiencing and enjoying it in their own backyards. Presenting your features and benefits with a running tub will be easier and far more effective than just staring at an empty spa and repeating over and over "Imagine this or imagine that."

The sights and sounds of a running spa are relaxing to your prospect. It helps create the perfect oasis they are hoping to achieve in their own backyard. A fully loaded hot tub as your running model, as opposed to a basic bare bones model, is an incredibly valuable tool to help you sell additional options and features. It is more effective to have your prospect mentally remove features they are not interested in, than asking them to mentally add features they may want.

If you are working with an empty spa, how can you:

- Effectively demonstrate your stunning lighting package as it illuminates the water?

- Paint the picture of your prospect enjoying the massaging action of the jets when they can't feel anything?

- How can you Effectively demonstrate those waterfalls and see your prospects' reaction as they hold their hands under the warm water?

- How do you Paint the picture of a relaxing dip in the spa on a cold February night?

- Trying to "up-sell" a stereo on a spa which can be challenging on a good day - Try selling a stereo as an add-on if you are using a basic bare bones spa without a stereo. "Mr. Prospect, just imagine how nice this would be if you could listen to your favourite music," just won't cut it.

Would you agree it would be far more effective if you had a loaded running spa, with all the bells and whistles, while you had your prospect adjusting the volume levels on the music, perhaps with a remote control?

I think it should go without saying that in the absence of a running spa, your prospect will wonder why you don't have one, when your competitor does. You may lose credibility in your prospects' eyes, and never know it.

Hopefully, all your spas on display are clean and spotless, free of dust, coffee rings and especially water spots on your running spa. Your spas should be clear of any item that would prevent your prospect from hopping in. The water in your running spa must be crystal clear and also smell clean. If your water is cloudy and it smells like a science lab, what do you think your prospect will be thinking about your product? Would you buy a car if it was covered in mud and the ashtray overflowing with cigarette butts and the back seat full of fast food wrappers?

Inventory, Know Thyself

Is your inventory knowledge strong or do you run around your store looking for specific spas? Have you committed to memory exactly which models are on display, where they are located and what features and options each has?

Do you scratch your head and wonder where the eight-foot white lounger went from the back corner, and when? Walk your show-room floor every single day to refresh your memory of everything you have on display and which spas have been sold or delivered. Have you attached bold SOLD signs to your spas that have been purchased, but not yet delivered? Make the sold sign personal; include the family name of the purchaser (with permission of course). A "Sold to the happy Johnson family" sign can be very powerful to motivate your prospect. They are especially useful if you have a "be-back" that has returned to look at a spa, which has now been sold. In the unlikely event your customer doesn't want their name on your sold sign, simply use a generic sign, "Sold to another happy family" or "Sold to another satisfied owner."

Do you know what inventory you have in the back of your store? Do you know what spas are arriving next week? If you know what you have, where it is and the prices, you can easily guide your prospect into purchasing one of the spas you currently have on hand. How helpful would that knowledge be when your prospect says, "I'll buy it if you can deliver it on Thursday?"

How your spas are physically laid out on your showroom floor is extremely important. If you have a larger store with many models on display, arrange them in a logical order by grouping similar models next to each other so you and your prospect can do a side-by-side comparison of the interior layouts. Model ABC with a lounger should be next to model ABC without a lounger, not 25 feet away. Are your acrylic and siding samples neatly displayed or are they sitting in a dusty box with old "O rings" and other assorted spare parts? Do you have your most expensive spas front and centre? That may "sticker shock" your prospect; consider placing your basic models towards the front of your store so the first price the prospects see (assuming you use price tags) may easily fit in their budget. Ever had a pros-pect walk into your store, see a couple of very high price tags and leave? You may have "sticker shocked" them if they have just seen a $4,000 spa at a box store. Consider arranging your spas so they move up in price as you move farther into your store.

When presenting, I like to move back and forth between the various models so the prospect doesn't get bored of standing in one spot, shifting from one leg to the other. Keep a keen eye on their body language. Are they leaning in to you or keeping their distance with arms crossed? Keep them moving and keep them interested. As you read through this chapter, stand next to the spa you normally like to demo and do a practice presentation using what you have read. Remember to make this presentation yours. Use your words, thoughts and ideas - you own it. Use my suggestions as a script or guideline, memorize verbatim if you wish, but you absolutely don't want it to sound like a canned presentation.

Demonstration Bench

Do you have a demonstration bench? Have you ever used a demonstration bench? If you have one, do you use it as a selling tool? If you don't have one, why don't you? Having and using a demo bench is a surefire way to build value and reduce the chances of you data dumping.

Following your discovery, move your prospects over to your demo bench. A good demonstration bench should have samples of the key components that are in your spas. These are usually components neither you or your prospect will usually see if you look at a spa, such as manifolds, filters, plumbing samples, shell samples and perhaps an ozone generator. Displaying the various components of your spas, along with their associated benefits, will only help to increase your prospects' perceived value of your products.

Think of your demonstration bench as a method to start building value by giving your prospect a "look under the hood." Show your prospect examples of your pumps, jets, plumbing and manifold assemblies, shell cut-a-ways, insulation, and the electronics. Your bench may even include a stereo and a remote control system. Don't forget to tie the features of the bench components into benefit statements. If your products have a completely unique feature, have a sample of it on your demo bench and focus on the benefits this unique feature will provide.

Personally, I have never been a big fan of putting a heavy emphasis on the technical components of any product; I prefer to focus on selling to my prospects needs and dreams which are rarely technical in nature That being said and used in moderation, a demo bench is a great opportunity to differentiate yourself from your competition. Very few hot tub stores have a demo bench, let alone use it effectively. You can easily use your demo bench as a starting point for your presentation following your discovery. During your FAB statements of the various components, you should start to get feedback from your prospect as to what is, and what is not, important to them (always lots of questions, remember you have permission to ask questions). After a brief review of your various spa components, you should be able to comfortably start your presentation.

> *"Mr. Prospect, there are really only a few key considerations when you are shopping for a spa."*

Of course, every manufacturer will have their own unique features, here are a few key areas to focus on:

1. Shell

> *"Mr. Prospect, the spa shell is the area of the spa you see. This is where you will actually be sitting. (If you have small vacuum formed samples, this is even more effective. Have a sample of a thinly formed shell and another sample with a shell with fibreglass reinforcing.) Most shells are vacuum formed and when finished, are very thin (hand them the shell sample without fibreglass). Reinforcing the shell is critical. After the shells are formed, they are heavily reinforced with fibreglass (now exchange the sample they are*

holding for the reinforced sample). We use... (insert your specific structural reinforcing details here, remembering to not only mention the method you use, by what the benefit to the prospects is). As a result of our manufacturing process and fibreglass reinforcing, we can offer a lifetime warranty against leaks (use the specifics of your warranty)."

You can easily drop a trial close in here. "Mr. Prospect, how would you feel knowing your spa had a lifetime warranty against shell leakage?"

"Mr. Prospect, usually the two biggest considerations when it comes to shell design are the layout, lounger or non-lounger and the seating capacity. How many people do you antici-pate using your hot tub? The shell color is usually one of the last considerations; these of course are strictly aesthetic."

"Are you considering a lounger or non-lounger design?"

2. Pumps and Jets

"Another consideration is your pumping and jetting require-ments. What do you need the spa to do for you? If you are more interested in a deep muscle massage for therapeutic reasons, I'll show you some of our larger pump and jetting packages. If you're leaning towards more of a fun soaker tub, you don't need to spend the money on larger pumps and more jets. We have just the right package for you and your family's needs."

3. Insulation

To Foam or Not to Foam
Are your spas full-foam, no-foam or partial-foam? This aspect of manufacturing always results in a lively debate, depending on

what you sell. This is not the forum to debate which one is best, rather how best to present the spa you sell. You will all know the pros of selling your unique manufacturing process. How well you present it is what will separate you from your competitors.

You *must* explain the different insulating options and explain why you believe yours is superior. Don't badmouth your competition, but by all means point out the weakness or perceived drawbacks of your competitor's insulation. Failing to mention the other insulation methods will come back to haunt you if your prospect decides to shop around, or already has, they will be curious why you never mentioned the other methods, and then wonder what else you deliberately chose not to mention.

> *"Mr. Prospect, there are a couple of different methods to insulate the underside of the spa. I'd like to take a minute to explain the different manufacturing methods and explain why we feel the _____ method is superior."*

Full-Foam

> *"Mr. Prospect, insulating the underside of the spa is crucial. The industry standard is called Full-Foam. This means the entire underside of the spa, other than the pumps and electronics, is filled with foam to eliminate any dead air spaces. What this means to you is threefold.*

> *"Firstly, the insulation value under the spa is increased dramatically compared with an empty air space. The result is lower operating costs associated with keeping the spa water hot.*

> *"Secondly, a sound-proofing affect results. When the underside is not foamed, the open air spaces act as a huge echo chamber and the sounds of the running pumps will be greatly amplified.*

"Thirdly, full-foam can extend the life of your spa. Your pumps will be turned on and off thousands of times over the life of your spa. Water flowing through the plumbing has movement. Think of firefighters when they turn a hose on - it takes two or three of them to hold it steady. This water movement is called the hammer effect."

Have a sealed 5-foot long 2-inch diameter hose two-thirds full of water and hand it to your prospect.

"Mr. Prospect, this is a sample of the plumbing under a spa. You can feel it is very heavy. Now hold one end of the hose; your hand represents the jet. Can you feel what the strain on the jet would be? Now, I will jiggle the hose to simulate the hammer effect. What do you think? You see, Mr. Prospect, full foam really does add structural support to the hoses and decreases the possibility of any potential leaks by 'locking' those hoses in place and reducing movement. Some spa manufacturers believe the exact opposite; they leave the foam out, which is cheaper to produce, and when it DOES leak, it is easier to fix. Which makes more sense to you – full-foam or no-foam? If dead air insulates so well, go home and remove all the insulation from your walls, put the dry wall back up and see if your next power bill is lower."

Partial or No-Foam

"Mr. Prospect, as much as all salespeople would love to say their spas don't leak, over time it is a reality that leaks will occur and those leaks will need to be serviced. Servicing a conventional full-foam spa can be a lot of work and can be quite expensive after the warranty period has lapsed. It is often a long diagnostic procedure in determining just exactly what and where the leakage problem is; this can be a costly adventure for you. With the entire underside of the

spa, and all the important plumbing joints and fittings encased in water-soaked foam, you could be looking at some very expensive service calls to repair any leaks. In the event you decide your spa needs to be serviced to find the leak, the spa is usually disconnected from the electrical supply, which means added costs to you, and flipped on its side. Only then does the laborious process of pulling out all the wet and smelly foam in search of the leak begin.

"In the event this method is unsuccessful in finding the leak, oftentimes the spa needs to be returned to the shop, where it is filled with colored water and a leak test performed to determine the leak's location. This procedure can take hours or even days. In a worst case scenario, the spa may need to be shipped back to the manufacturer and this cost can often be the owner's responsibly, depending on the spa warranty."

"The spa is then again drained and the repairs are completed. Following this, it is refilled again with colored water, to determine if the repair was successful."

"It is difficult enough to find any leak, but can you imagine having to find and fix the leak when everything in sight is covered in huge gobs of soaking wet and smelly insulation? So just how does one find a leak in foam that is soaking wet? Great question. You start by pulling out handfuls of wet foam in search of that elusive leak. After the leak has finally been located, isolated and repaired, the gaping hole is stuffed back with the old wet smelly foam. In some cases, new foam is pushed into the void. In a worse case scenario, no insulation is replaced. It is not uncommon to hear spa owners, with full-foam spas, put up with their leaks rather than spend the big bucks for the repair."

"Doesn't it make more sense to own a spa that offers complete access to all the crucial plumbing components, through *easy access panels? Can you imagine having the hood of your car welded shut? How easy would routine car maintenance be if that were the case?"*

Explain how the heat produced from the pumps is not wasted, but actually used to heat the spa. In the unlikely event of a power outage, the heat from the large body of water acts to protect the important components of the spa like plumbing lines and the pumps themselves from freezing.

"Operating costs can often be much lower in a spa that doesn't have full-foam, as the heat generated from the pumps serves to heat the underside of the spa. It doesn't make much sense to waste all that extra heat, does it?"

"Full-foam insulation can also provide a great nesting area for rodents and insects, especially in the winter as they search out a warm and comfortable home. Rodents have been known to chew through electrical wiring with ease."

4. Filtration

As you know, there are generally two schools of thought on filtration; 24-hour circulation pumps or running a jet pump on low speed for predetermined cycles. Your filtration presentation, much like your insulation presentation, will really depend on your product and what it offers.

Again, comment on the various methods of filtration that are available in your market, and having a good explanation as to why your system is superior to your competitor's offer is the key to your filtration presentation. I have given a few examples below of what some spa dealers will say to promote both filtration methods; the information you use and how you use it is entirely your choice. I am simply providing the different rebuttals I have heard.

Circulation Pump

"Mr. Prospect, one of the advantages of our 24-hour circulation pump is it provides continuous filtration 24/7. Other spa manufacturers choose to run their big expensive pumps on a low speed setting for their filtration needs, which is a lot like sending a man to do a boy's job.

"One of the advantages of using a dedicated circulation pump is that it is completely independent and doesn't cause any extra wear and tear on the big expensive pumps. Those big pumps are far more expensive and noisy to run and they still don't provide you with 24 hours a day filtration. Is continuously filtered clean water important to you and your wife?"

Many salespeople sell against a circulation pump (many shops will intentionally have an older-style, small volume, circulation pump on display), with the argument that circulation pumps are tiny little pumps, with very minimal water movement and as small as 1/15th of a horsepower, only able to turn the water over one or two times in a 24-hour period. Truth in advertising. You decide, as this may be what you are up against if your competitor is promoting low speed jet pumps for filtration.

Low-Speed Jet Pump

"Mr. Prospect, just one of the reasons we don't use circulation pumps in any of our spas is the spa owner usually doesn't have the flexibility to adjust the time duration of the filtering cycles, which really should be based on bather load. Filtering the water 24 hours a day is not only overkill, it just is not cost effective.

"For example, you don't need the water filtering between

1:00 a.m. and 6:00 a.m. when there is no one using the spa, do you? By using a jet pump on its lowest setting, your pumps will move far more water volume through the filters than a tiny little circulation pump ever will, and at the times you want it filtering."

Replaceable Filters

"Mr. Prospect, think of filtration this way: the filter cleans what your eyes can see (of course, it really filters particles much smaller than what the human eye can see) and the spa sanitizers clean what your eyes can't see."

Compare your filter size to your competitor's. You will also want to bring up your filter's micron size or what makes them unique. If you are selling against competition with many large expensive filters compared to yours, share that info. What is the expected life of their filter and what is the expected cost of changing three, four or even more filters every couple of years?

If you are selling against a competitor that claims to filter down to some amazingly small particle size, less than one micron, check with your local municipality as many municipalities only filter down to 10 microns for drinking water.

"Mr. Prospect, do you really need water filtered more than the water we drink?"

Discuss filter cleaning. Does your store offer filter cleaning as a service? This is a great way to get your prospects back in the store, point out premature wear and tear on the filters and up-sell more products.

After you have covered of the basics of shells, pumps and jets, insulation and filtration, you should now be ready to show some of your beautiful spas.

> *"Mr. Prospect, any guesses what the very first two considerations are when purchasing one of our spas? Well, usually most people focus on the shell design and the size. Shell design simply means the internal layout. Spas are usually built with or without a lounger, think of it as 'bench' type seating in the absence of a lounger. Size, as we discussed earlier, will be determined by your physical space requirements and the number of bathers you see enjoying the spa."*

Move your prospect to the appropriate spa you think will fit their needs.

> *"So, this is an example of what we were talking about earlier (you would have learned during discovery about their lounger or bench style seating preferences), this is the ABC model with a lounger and this spa next to it has upright or bench style seats (move them back and forth between the two models). Other than the lounger feature, think of these two models as a brother and sister to each other.*
>
> *"A spa with the lounger design not only allows you to lay out flat and recline, you also receive the added benefit of having massage jets work directly on the backs of your legs. If you are a skier, a cyclist, a jogger or a sports enthusiast, this is a terrific design. If you are like me, this is my favourite place in the spa; my wife prefers the bench-style seating. This design is perfect for my family as we don't end up fighting for a favourite seat. It really is a personal preference. You mentioned earlier that a _____ (lounger or bench) arrangement would work best for you. How do you feel about this layout?"*

Where do you physically position yourself when presenting a spa, in respect to your prospects' position? Proper positioning is very important. Stand off to one side so your prospects are together, and front and centre to your demo is always my first choice. Try to never stand in between them as it makes it very difficult to talk and maintain eye contact with both of prospects at the same time. You should always be watching for any subtle little clues such as body language changes. If you are in between them, they are a divided couple. They are physically separated and it is very easy for them to nod, wink or make gesturers to each other that you are unaware of.

Those unseen gestures may be positive, perhaps a thumbs up from the partner you don't see or a head shaking and adamant "no" from the other. You are in control - use that control and suggest where they should stand for maximum effect as you present your spas. Ask them, "What is the first thing you notice about our spas?"

Point out all the immediate visual features and differences they will notice between your spa and your competitor's spas. Your spas may be similar; if they are not, focus on the unique features of your spas that are visually apparent.

Focus on Unique Features

Here are a few examples:

Built-In Steps

If you have built-in steps, point them out, as they are a huge selling feature. If not, try to imagine how you would focus on one of your unique spa features.

"That is correct, Mr. Prospect, all our spas have built-in steps. The XYZ Spa Company is one of the only hot tub manufacturers that care enough about your family's safety

to build steps in. This may not be important to everybody; you and I can probably hop in and out of the spa with little effort or risk. But if you have older parents like I do (mom is 82 and dad is 85), or younger kids, you might be setting someone up for a bad fall on a wet surface without these steps. It isn't just getting into the spa that can be difficult - without steps most people end up doing the 'leap of faith' into the deep end (point out how they would enter a non-stepped spa by stepping down on to a deep seat, a possible drop of over two feet). Would you also agree getting out of the spa safely is important?"

Your prospect may have no idea of what it feels like getting in or out of a spa. Explain that exiting the spa, after 30 minutes of deep relaxation, and perhaps a few cold beverages, can be the challenging. Share with them that getting grandma out of the spa is often the time when many people can easily take a tumble if they don't have the benefit of built-in steps.

"Is keeping Grandma safe when she uses the spa important to you and your family?"

Handrail

If you have an "easy grip" edge or triple rail, point it out along with its benefits.

"Notice the wraparound handrail on our spas? In the XX years the XYZ spa company has been building spas, they have learned to include a couple of features most people would never consider if they have never owned a spa. Feel how easy it is to grip. Would this help your family members feel more secure when they moved around the spa? Now imagine no handrail, a wet surface and darkness. What do you think might happen?"

Foot Well

"Another key feature when looking for a hot tub is a large foot well. This is that area where you need ample room, especially if the men are coming over. Men often have a thing about touching any body part of another man, especially anything below the waist, like their feet. I love my brother very much, but I still don't want him touching my feet and I am sure he feels the same way. With a larger foot well, you also have a nice flat surface for your feet when you stand up to exit or just move around in the spa."

Getting in the Hot Tub

Many salespeople tell me they have difficulty getting their prospects into a dry demo tub. "Get in the hot tub, Mr. Prospect" doesn't work very well. The most effective way I have found to encourage your prospects to "hop in the tub" is by combining direction and curiosity.

As you take your shoes off (or keep them on depending on your store policy), simply lead by example.

"Hop in here with me for a minute, as there's something I want to show you."

Up to this point, you will have been setting the pace, taking control and guiding their direction - why stop now? Lead by example. In mentioning, "There is something I want to show you," you will have piqued their curiosity. You should have had enough enthusiasm and control to get 9 out of 10 people into the spa (in the unlikely event they decline your invitation, don't worry about it - get in and continue).

"Now that we are in the spa, how does that feel? Are you comfortable? Stretch your legs out and relax. So would you

like a glass of red wine or sparkling apple juice? This is that new dehydrated spa, just add water."

Corny comment, yes, but very effective in getting them laughing.

"Mr. Prospect, it is crucial for you to get into a dry spa to test the fit, as many spas look nice from the outside, but it is only when you actually get in that you might find the legroom is very restrictive, you may be too tall for the spa or discover there are jets jabbing you in the back. Oftentimes, you will find the spa really doesn't fit you as well as it looked like it would."

This is a very powerful technique to eliminate the spas often sold at box stores or in the classified ads:

"Big box stores often keep their spas on their side as this prevents you from sitting in them to check the fit.

"Now that we're all here in the tub, here is what I wanted to show you. This is where the water level would be when the tub is full of bubbly warm water."

Show them, without touching them, where the waterline would be.

"Can you imagine what a deep soak up to your shoulders would feel like in January on a cold rainy / snowy night (always be painting those mental pictures)? Mr. Prospect, which seat do you think would be your favourite? Why is that? Which seats do you think your kids would enjoy the most? Why? Now take a moment to look around the spa, you will notice every seat or 'jetting station' has a different jet configuration. Older spas used to have only a few jets, all aimed at the same spot. After five minutes, many people

*complained they got really itchy. The old tubs were great at
inflating your swimsuit and tickling your bum, but that was
about all."*

If you feel your prospects are a wee bit prude or standoffish, you
may not want to use that last line. Nine times out of ten, your prospects will relate to it and laugh, because it was true.

*"Today, the XYZ spa company works directly with chiroprac-
tors and other health care professionals in designing our
jet placement. What this means to you is maximum muscle
relaxation. You spend five minutes in each seat relaxing a
different set of muscles, so at the end of a 30 minute soak
all your major muscle groups are totally relaxed. Does that
sound like something you might enjoy?"*

At this point, your prospect has felt the comfort of your dry spa,
confirmed the legroom and the fit, tried the different seat configurations, and visualized themselves enjoying their spa with their
family on a cold winter evening. There is no better time than now
to touch on some features and benefits. The longer they sit with
you in the spa, the more likely they will take ownership in their
minds. They are mentally transferring their showroom experience
to their own backyards.

Point Out What They See

There is no better time than right now to start mentioning all the
features of your spa that they can see and touch, and the benefit
each delivers.

*"Mr. Prospect, these are our 'easy adjust' jets. Just give them
a turn and see for yourself just how easy they are to adjust.
Pretty smooth aren't they? The nice thing is even grandma*

or your younger kids can easily adjust them to their personal preference."

"Mr. Prospect, as you look around the spa, notice each seat has a different jetting package. Each jet has a very specific massaging action. This particular jet is a cluster or 'bullet jet,' which delivers a hard straight stream of water much like pushing a finger deep into a sore muscle (demonstrate with your hands the massaging action of the various jets - you can be VERY animated with this, even to the point of being overly dramatic)."

Describe each of the different jets they see and their associated benefits, as your prospect is watching. Use animated gestures with your hands, twisting, chopping, rubbing palms together, etc. Paint the picture. Are your jets interchangeable? Share that useful information and the other benefits of having a customizable spa.

"How would you feel after a long hard stressful day at the office when you finally get home and lean back into a hot, pulsating massage on your sore neck?"

Use all the information you gathered during your discovery and hand it back to them with the benefits they will receive. If they mentioned having a sore neck, focus on it. If they want the spa for family entertainment, focus on how large and spacious the interior is, perfect for friends and family. You will be more successful in closing if you constantly keep them involved. Are you starting to see why having a great discovery is so valuable? Now imagine trying to create an effective demonstration without having completed a thorough discovery.

"Mr. Prospect, if this exact model was in your backyard tonight, of course full of nice hot bubbling water, perhaps with you enjoying a frosty beverage or two, what would be your view from the lounger? It sounds like the lounger will be your

favourite seat (positive assumptions they will purchase). Where do you think the kids would sit? What would your kids think if this spa was in your backyard? Many families never realized the quality family time that results from having a hot tub or pool in the backyard. Parents often share with me that it is during their weekly 'family spa session,' without the distraction of TV, cellphones ringing, computers and video games, that they get to really connect with their kids and find out how things really are. Much like with a road trip in a car, the hot tub environment often results in great conversations and family time."

Demonstrating Your Running Spa

Here is where you will get your prospects' biggest "OOOOOH" and "AHHHHH" moments of your entire presentation. The effective demonstration of your running tub is a very powerful part of your presentation. Use it wisely, as you only get to make your first impression once.

"Mr. Prospect, do you want to really have some fun? Let me show you what all the features and these different jets we discussed really mean to you and your family."

It is time to get them to move from your dry tub and over to your running model. More often than not, the woman is left to climb out of the spa, unassisted by her partner. Be a pro and make it easier for her, be respectful and offer a hand, as chivalry and courtesy are not dead. If you are a man and this sounds silly to you, go ask your spouse, your sister or any female member of your staff what their opinion is. It is these little niceties the lovely women in our lives NOTICE, at least that is what my wife tells me.

Try to remember your body positioning as you approach the running tub. Always have a couple of dry towels nearby for them to place any jewellery they don't wish to get wet and to dry their hands on.

Drying their hands on the robes hanging next to your running tub or worse yet, on their pant legs, is pretty unprofessional. I hope that doesn't sound too familiar to you.

When and how your prospect experiences their first interaction with your running spa is a HUGE moment. If you prepare for and present it effectively, you will never get a bigger "OOOOOH" and "AHHHHH" moment than when they initially put their hands in front of the running jets. That is the second time I've said that - maybe I should mention it just one more time. I think you get the idea of the importance. Here is where you need to paint a great picture in advance of them getting wet. Put them in the right moment, in their minds, in their backyard.

You can certainly present this moment with great playful pomp and ceremony, if that is your style - it is mine. Have them roll up their sleeves and hold their hands just above the water. At this point the spa pumps should be off (soothing music playing is okay), you should have tested well in advance (ideally during your morning walk around your spas, as you do everyday) that all the jets of your running spa are open for a full blast and have the air controls wide open to create the most vigorous massage action possible.

> *"Mr. Prospect, we could talk about jets, pumps and plumbing all day, but this is what all that technology really means to you."*

Turn all the pumps on to maximum. You may even take advantage of one of their kids and have them press the buttons. You should already be very familiar with which jets each of the pumps control and know which seats are affected by the diverter controls and which jets the various air controls affect.

> *"Imagine for a minute, Mr. Prospect, it is January. It is cold,
> damp and hasn't stop snowing or raining for five days. How
> does your back/neck/hip feel on days like that? Now please
> slide your hand in front of the jets."*

Shut up and let them speak first. Watch and listen to their reaction.
Remember the ice trucker? Often this is where a buying signal will
surface, so be ready for it.

> *"I can see by your reaction that this really wouldn't feel very
> good after all, would it? All kidding aside, how does that
> feel? Please go on. How would that feel on your sore neck
> Mr. Prospect (substitute any of the 'hot buttons' you learned
> during your discovery)?"*

Have them feel and experience the different jetting effects, ask
them which are their favourites and why. Get them turning and twisting all the jets on and off and activating the pumps like they own it.
Make this a fun, dynamic and engaging moment for both you and
your prospect. Be passionate and enthusiastic. Walk them through
the basic functions of the spa like the keypad, air controls and the
diverter. Explain that each jet (assuming you have adjustable jets) is
fully adjustable. Can you identify the WIIFM with adjustable jets?

I loved having a big family to present to. Try to get every family
member actively involved in you presentation. Make them a part of
it - help them own it. Have the spouse or kids turn on the pumps
or adjust the diverter. How important do you think they would feel
being involved?

If you are working with mom, dad and the kids, the kids can be
your most effective selling tool. Keeping the kids interested, engaged and entertained will prevent mom and dad from having to
take their restless kids home only to interrupt your presentation
and delay their purchase until later. Think on your feet. You can

drop in a HUGE trial close following their comments after their hands entered the water, if you feel the reaction was strong.

> *"Mr. Prospect, judging by your reaction, it sure looks like you would like to have one of our spas. Why don't we just go pick one out and then I can stop talking and you can start enjoying?"*

Try this close if you have built up a strong rapport. At times, my prospect has agreed and we selected a spa right then and there, or they have replied with, "Hang on, we're not there yet." My selling style is based on humour and is a very playful interaction that allows me a lot of freedom in how I present, ask my trial closes, and sell. You will find your own path, with practice. After a huge buying signal, I have often simply said, "Will the deposit be a cheque or credit card?" As I always assume they will buy from me, it is up to them to tell me "No" or "We're not quite there, yet." You need to be trial closing throughout your presentation so by the time you come to the end of your presentation, nobody is shocked or surprised that you have asked for the sale!

Explain that your spa company manufacturers *custom* built spas to suit their individual needs.

> *"Folks, one of the most common comments our owners share with us is that by us building or customizing the spa for them, they didn't end up paying for features or accessories they would never want or use. Does that make sense to you?*

> *"In my family, I enjoy the lounger for the leg jets; my wife carries her stress in her neck and prefers the dedicated neck jets."*

Explain wrist jets, power domes and all the different packages you offer with your spas. Something as simple as wrist jets may make all the difference to your prospect if they spend most of their day hunched over a computer.

*"Mr. Prospect, the XYZ spa company only uses the most **energy efficient, quality, high-flow pumps** in their design. Our pumps, combined with an engineered plumbing design, deliver up to XXX GPM more water than other spas on the market. What this means to you is a more vigorous massage, lower operating costs and a much quieter spa. Can you imagine how frustrating it would be to sit in your spa and have to shout over the noise of the pumps to talk to your spouse or kids? Many spa companies focus on the horsepower of their pumps, they need these large pumps with huge horsepower because their pumps and plumbing are very inefficient. All horsepower ratings are not the same; there is Break HP, Running HP, and Continuous HP. Get your hands in front of the working jets and YOU decide which feels better."*

"Each and every one of our spas is water tested at the factory for a minimum of two hours (or whatever your particular brand tests). Many spa manufacturers only water test every tenth spa." (What would you add as the benefit statement to this feature?)

"Remember we discussed the older spas from years ago? They were very basic and simple in design and technology. After a five-minute soak, your skin started feeling really itchy. What caused your skin feel itchy was the amount of air coming out of the jet with the water. Feel this (your prospects' hands should be on the jets while you adjust the air control). You see by adding or removing air, YOU can adjust the intensity of the massage you receive. Does that sound like something you would like on your spa?"

Are you getting a handle on what it takes to have a dynamite presentation? Does it make sense to mention a feature, turn it into an advantage and then, most importantly, into a benefit, and then ask if that benefit makes sense to your prospects' lifestyle? When you finally get to price presentation, you will be able to give all this knowledge and your benefit confirmations back to your prospect, especially when they say, "I need to think about it."

A great spa presentation should include a good overview of the spa's various components and the benefits the prospect will receive. For more specific technical details as they pertain to your particular brand or product, check with your printed product literature, store management or the manufacturer's representative. You need to understand your product's USP. Learn what your competitor is selling, how they are selling it and what they are saying - not just about their products, but your products as well.

The small list of features that follows MUST be committed to memory for an effective presentation of your hot tubs. Adjust your presentation to reflect your products and your specifics. You will find your own presentation style and order; vary the order and content of your information to suit you and your presentation style. You own your presentation and it should be as unique as you are. You don't have to mention all the technical components in the spa and your spa's unique manufacturing process, but be prepared to integrate the key features and the benefits that result in meeting and exceeding your prospects' needs.

1. CEC

"Mr. Prospect, all our spas meet the California Energy Commission (CEC) requirements in accordance with California law. What this means to you is in being CEC compliant, it ensures you our spas have the greatest energy efficiency and have the least environmental impact."

2. CONTOURED SEATING

Explain that contoured seating will provide the user with a much more comfortable experience than an upright and angular seating layout found in many cheaper tubs.

> *"Many manufacturers strive for maximum seating in exchange for maximum comfort in their spas."*

Share with your prospect that your spas have a variety of different seating designs and jetting layouts specifically designed so that they can enjoy an incredible variety of massages as they move around the spa. It's amazing how people move around in their spas and don't just sit in one seat for the entire time. The different seats enable your prospect to enjoy a variety of jet configurations that massage their back, shoulders, neck, etc. at different angles. Have them think of their spa experience as a game of musical chairs, with each seat providing relaxation for a different set of muscles.

3. COVERS

Again, like most products, your manufacturers' covers may be unique. Do you understand what makes yours special or different? Is it sun and UV resistant? Can it support a heavy snow load or someone walking on it? Does it have an R-rating or insulation value? When selling or promoting covers, compare your R-value to their home insulation R-values; the average home has an R-rating of R18-28 on external walls. This simple comparison helps your prospect understand the comparison far easier than hearing a long list of facts and figures.

If your cover is tapered, mention the benefit that it aids in rain runoff. What are the internal structural components of your covers, or are there any? If you are selling against "off-shore" spas, they generally lack a strong internal structure or a high R-value. How long is your cover warranty? Explain the high costs associated with replacing a cheap cover. Do your covers have any locking straps for safety? (This is a great selling tool if your prospect has young children and safety concerns.) The list is long as far as selling covers go; know your covers, the advantages yours offers AND the advantages and disadvantages of your competitor's covers. Are your handles double-stitched and reinforced? Can your prospect select color options?

4. COVER LIFTERS

Can you easily name the various types of lifters you promote and the advantages of one brand versus another?

5. ELECTRICAL ISSUES AND PAD REQUIREMENTS

Electrical and pad costs and requirements need to be addressed up front and not ignored. Not disclosing these important budget concerns will bite you in the butt more than it will help you. Your prospects will see you as the true professional if you give them the straight goods on the all the costs associated with owning a hot tub. The investment costs are more then just the tub. Be honest and tell them in advance they will most likely need a dedicated electrical GFI circuit breaker for their tubs. They will also need to make sure the pad they put down follows the spa manufacturer's recommendations, as not to void the warranty. Depending on your state or province or country, there may also be required permit issues.

6. ENGINEERING

Explaining how your hot tubs are manufactured can answer many concerns your prospect may have, but doesn't share with you. They may have misguided beliefs in the lack of quality of your product. This may have come from reading online hot tub chat groups or even negative comments made by your competitor. Many companies design the mold and decide where the jets should be placed for maximum massage therapy, which is optimized at 12 – 14 PSI at the smaller jets and 9 – 11 PSI at the larger jets. Following this, they then size the motors and pumps accordingly to ensure there is 9 - 14 PSI at each jet. Limiting the number of 90-degree elbows in plumbing also helps to reduce the required horsepower rating to achieve the desired PSI.

7. FILTRATION FOCUS

> *"Mr. Prospect, it is all about clean and clear water - just ask any woman in your life. Most men are happy to get into warm water with a cold beer, even if the spa water is cloudy or smells funky. Most women usually won't go near a spa unless it is crystal clear and smells pristine."*

Expand this point to your prospect. How many times per day does the water go through the filters if no one uses the tub? How many times per hour when the jets are on HIGH? With a circulation pump, continuous water movement "cycles" the entire contents of the tub, in some cases in as little as 15 minutes - that's about 100 times each day! If you don't sell circulation pumps, explain the benefits of using a main pump on low speed.

8. THE BENEFITS OF YOUR MICRO FILTER SYSTEM

Explain to your prospect that either directly or eventually, all the water goes through the filter. The filter cartridge catches anything larger than XX microns, which is far smaller than the dot of a pencil. How small of a particle does your filter system catch? Depending on your geographical location, the average city drinking water is filtered down to 10 microns. Why filter less than that?

A great way of explaining filters is to explain that the skimmer basket and the filter trap the things you can see, while the sanitizers kill the things you can't see.

If your spa has a filter that catches down to one micron, pitch that you go above and beyond the cleanliness of city water.

9. THE EASE OF FILTER CLEANING AND CHANGES

Explain to your prospect what will be involved in the maintenance of their tub and the filters. Show them how easy it is to remove the filter, spray it with a garden hose and replace it. Many spa owners believe it is best to cycle their filters, bringing one set into the garage to dry for the next month; they think it will last longer than continual use of one set of filters and that this "down time" will allow them to soak the filters in filter cleaners without interrupting the enjoyment of the tub. Here is a great opportunity to up-sell them on a filter cleaning service, if you offer it.

10. FILTRATION WITH CIRCULATION PUMP OR LOW-SPEED PUMP

Most manufacturers either promote a circulation pump or a pump on low speed for filtration. The benefits of each filtering method are up to you to present to your prospect. Understand and be able to explain the differences, as it can be a major selling point when your prospect is deciding between your spas AND your competition.

CIRCULATION PUMP

A circulation pump is a small independent pump that is solely responsible for circulating the water through the filters, 24 hours a day, 7 days a week. They often require minimal electrical consumption and usually have low noise transfer.

LOW-SPEED JET PUMP

Explain how a jet pump on a low speed can have a low-amp rating and this may result in a more cost-effective method of filtration when compared with some 24-hour filtering of a circulation pump. Advantages may include the option to adjust the filtration cycles based on bather loads. Some manufacturers will say their low-speed pump moves more water through the filters in a given cycle than a small circulation pump moves in 24 hours.

11. FILLING AND EMPTYING THE SPA

Many prospects that have never owned a spa may have no idea if there are any external plumbing requirements, concerns or issues. Explain that you simply fill your tub with a garden hose (with or without a filter).

When you change the water, every three or four months, attach a garden hose to the drain (if equipped) and allow the water to drain away from the tub.

12. FOOT WELL

In our society, most people don't mind touching elbows or most any other body part above the waistline, but most people don't like touching the legs or feet of other people in the spa. Large foot wells allow your prospect to sit comfortably with plenty of foot and legroom when your friends or family are in the tub with you. We call it the "leg spaghetti" game in smaller spas with limited leg-room. The foot wells in some tubs are very small which may lead to a problem. In smaller tubs with limited foot room, bather's legs tend to stick much farther into and across the foot well of the spa, so you really can't get as many people in to enjoy the spa. It can also be uncomfortable when it's cold and windy out, as bathers often have to scrunch down in their seats to keep the water up to their shoulders and necks. If it's a six-person spa, it really needs to have sufficient room for six pairs of legs.

13. HEADRESTS OR BUILT-IN PILLOWS

"Mr. Prospect, acrylic isn't a very soft surface to lay your head against and relax. Many manufacturers place pillows in seats where you are more likely to lean your head against. When you lay back and relax in your spa, would you rather have a comfortable pillow to cushion your head as you relax and rest your head or a hard uncomfortable acrylic surface?"

14. DON'T HAVE PILLOWS ON YOUR TUBS?

Mention the advantages of "add-on" or after-market pillows and their ease of cleaning, coupled with their bacterial resistance, if that is what you sell. Get to know your pillows, but more importantly, know your competitor's warranty on their pillows and use it to your advantage. Some spa pillows only have a 90-day warranty. In the event you don't sell pillows with your spas, simply ask your prospect, "Why do you think many manufacturers only offer a 90-day warranty, Mr. Prospect?" You will instill a strong level of doubt in your prospects' mind regarding the quality of the competitor's pillows.

15. INTERIOR SPACE

> *"Mr. Prospect, when deciding on the perfect spa for your family, look at how much interior room you will actually have in the spa. Many manufacturers measure their spas externally, but it doesn't really tell you how much space you have when you're in the spa with your friends and family."*

Some salespeople will suggest when comparing similar models, compare the spa's water volume as a more accurate reflection of the internal size; these volumes are usually posted in US gallons.

Spend a moment and look at how wide the corner seats are, as some corners have what are called a "shallow radius," which means the corner seats are very narrow and constrictive, resulting in your prospects' back and shoulders being very confined. Imagine three or four people using the spa - how much room is there for standing up and moving around? If there is a jetted-foot dome, does it cover most of the floor, resulting in an uneven footing platform and difficulty standing "flat-footed?"

16. JETS

This topic has been broken into three sections: adjustable jets, interchangeable jets and recessed jets. Jet count is another area for discussion, depending on your manufacturer's counting meth-odology; some manufacturers count a cluster jet with nine open-ings as nine jets, when in fact it has only one jet body. If you are selling against a competitor whose spa has 300 jets (yes, slight sarcasm and exaggeration, although I have seen claims of 188 jets), find out how your competitors count their jets and be sure to explain this very important difference to your prospects.

- Adjustable Jets

  You may have none, some or all jets that are adjustable - what's in it for your prospect? Most jets are adjustable, simply by turning the face of the jet. You can turn it off completely or keep it completely open to allow maximum water flow. Explain to your prospects that if they desire more pressure from the jet behind them, turn off some of the jets in the unused seats and the extra pressure will increase the flow to the jets that remain open (assuming your spa has a suitable manifold system that allows this). What is the benefit of this feature to your prospect?

- Interchangeable Jets

  Many of the larger jets in hot tubs are interchangeable. Are yours? If so, do you know exactly which jets can be exchanged and what the benefits of each jet are? Can your prospect create a "custom designed" seat in their own tub by swapping the jets around?

- Recessed Jets

  Some spa manufacturers do not recess their jets. These jets may end up poking your prospect in the back and causing discomfort. This can be a sign of inferior manufac-turing. If you don't have recessed jets, explain how this is a benefit and actually brings the jets closer to your prospects skin for increased jet action. If you are selling spas with recessed jets, the pitch is very easy by focusing on the comfort of recessed jets and by explaining the extra costs the manufacturer has spent in their mold designs to ensure your prospects comfort and enjoyment.

As a general rule of thumb, many manufacturers will tell the prospect if a tub is not comfortable dry, it will not be comfortable wet. If your tubs are uncomfortable dry, focus on getting your prospects to take a wet test.

Share with your prospect that they are far more buoyant in water than on land, so spas tend to be very comfortable wet compared to dry.

17. LIP DESIGN

If your spa features a wraparound handrail or an "easy grip" lip, be sure to share the benefits of this great feature with your prospect or you will lose a very valuable selling feature and benefit. When your prospect uses their spa, water will naturally be splashed in, on and around the tub. A spa with a built-in handrail or "easy grip" design permits water to drip off and not collect on the edge. A safe grip ensures safer entry and exit and movement within the spa. Some manufacturers use low-grade metal "assist" bars inside their tubs that may rust or rip out of the spa after a few years of continued usage.

18. MANIFOLDS

Manifolds are a great plumbing feature that create an even water distribution within the tub. This results in an equal water flow to each of the various jets. This reduces excessive wear and tear on the jet components as compared to spa manufacturers that don't use manifolds. Spas plumbed with jets placed in series can't offer even water flow. What are the benefits of your particular manufacturer's manifolds? How can you use this information as a benefit in your presentation?

19. OPERATING COST

The average cost of electricity to run a high-quality hot tub is anywhere from $25 to $85 per month averaged throughout the year. Understand and explain to your prospects the energy testing your particular hot tub manufacturer has conducted and where the testing was carried out. Many spa companies carry out their testing in harsher climates like Canada. If you are working with a prospect that is energy conscious, this is a chance to shine. If you are comparing a Canadian-made brand to an "offshore" spa made in a warmer climate, you may have the opportunity to focus on the fact your spa was built in the climate it will be used in.

20. OZONE

Ozone, or O3, acts as a powerful oxidant and is used as a water sanitizer. It has been used successfully for over 100 years as a sanitizer. Using ozone allows the user to significantly reduce the amount of chemicals required to kill bacteria and other impurities in the spa. Your specific ozone details may be USPs, and if so, you may wish to focus on them during your presentation.

21. PACK AND HEATER

Explain the benefits of your pack (the brains) and heater (the muscle) as it compares to your competitors. You may have a hot tub that uses smart technology and adjusts the heating requirement based on heating requirements (1 kilowatt in low demand situations and 4+ kilowatt heating during high demand). Know the specifics of your pack and heater; understand what you sell and how that will benefit your prospect! You may also be asked to explain the heating times following a fresh cold fill or how fast your tub will heat when it is -10 outside with five people in the tub.

22. PUMP SIZE AND WATERFLOW

This is probably the one of the biggest areas of debate in the spa industry. There is a lot of disagreement about HORSEPOWER, what it really means and how it should be presented as it relates to hot tub performance. It often stems from the reality that there are many different ways to measure horsepower: a true horse-power rating, break horsepower, mechanical horsepower. The list is very long and often misunderstood, especially by your prospect.

Each manufacturer should present their position as to what their unique horsepower rating actually means to the end user. This is neither the time nor place for this discussion, as there are merits for each product offering. How you present the topic of horse-power will all depend on your store and the products you carry, as well as your competition. The key concept to keep in mind is how efficiently the pump power is used and what the end result will be: happy owners.

The motors and pumps used today are often smaller and more efficient motors then in years gone by. The best choice is a pump that will deliver excellent performance and use a lot less energy to do it. There is also great merit in the "It's all about the GPM at the jet" opinion. Many spa dealers will explain to the prospect their pumps provide - insert any number here - gallons of water at the jet. Many spa dealers that sell against GPM will switch the focus to horsepower and not on the water flow coming out of the jet. In the end, the goal is to have sufficient pressure at the jets to provide a therapeutic massage, without wasting the power of the pump. Get your prospect to get their hands in front of the running jets, nothing more need be said after that.

23. PLUMBING QUALITY

PVC, ABS or flexible pipe are just a few of the options available to spa manufacturers. Learn the quality and grade of plumbing in the spas you sell. Some manufacturers use cheaper hoses with garden-style hose clamps to secure the waterlines to the jets. These might work well for a few months, but then what? What can you share with your prospect in regards to your plumbing and how they will benefit?

24. SIDING

Is each one of your side panels removable? If so, explain the benefits to your prospect that in the unlikely event you need to service the spa, especially after the warranty has expired, it will be easier if you have access to the underside of the spa. If your customer does have a problem, your customer will most likely want the technician to be able to access the underside easily. Do you have synthetic siding? What are the benefits of this feature?

25. SHELL

Do you offer a LIFETIME guarantee that your shell will hold water? What is your policy on leakage? Do you share this important information with your prospect?

> *"Mr. Prospect, with our lifetime shell guarantee and our construction quality, you will never have to worry about your spa shell cracking and leaking water. How does that make you feel?"*

26. STEPS BUILT IN

Does your spa have the benefit of large integrated steps? If so, this is an easy feature to sell.

> *"Mr. Prospect, did you notice the size of our spa entry steps? Many bathers are often entering and exiting the spa at night. The larger the step, the safer it will be going in and out of your spa. The steps also double as cooling seats. When you've been in the spa for an extended period of time, you may wish to cool down a bit, but not wish to leave the company of your friends and family. You have the option of sitting on either of the top two steps, which is far safer than balancing on the edge of the spa and you still have the added benefit of keeping your legs and lower body in the warm water. Steps are also perfect seats for smaller children or grandchildren."*

Don't forget to focus on safety. *"Is Grandma safer entering the spa with steps or without steps?"*

27. NO STEPS

No worries - simply explain to your prospects that the lack of steps allows for more jetted seats, and entry and exit is still not compromised with a little due care and caution when entering from the edge of the tub.

28. STEREO

A stereo is a great addition to any spa. Focus on the relaxation aspects of having music when your prospect is enjoying their spa. Get creative when selling stereos - use it as an up-sell when presenting the available options.

29. UNIQUENESS

The USP of your product is its Unique Selling Proposition. Your spa will most likely have features and benefits that are completely unique to your competition. These are important items to focus on that will help build value in your prospects' mind. If they feel they absolutely have to have your spas features, and these features are completely unique to your spas, hearing, "We need to think about it" or "We need to shop around," should not be very difficult objections to overcome.

30. WARRANTY

Good warranties are pretty standard in the industry. If you have anything about yours that truly sets you apart from your competition, focus on it. Most standard warranties are three to five years - in some cases pro-rated, in some cases not. Is there anything unique about yours?

31. WATERFALLS AND LIGHTS

Waterfalls and lights are a wonderful addition to any spa. Share

with your prospect that waterfalls and lights are incredibly effective in relaxing their mind, while the therapeutic massaging jets in
the spa soothe their bodies. The feeling of a waterfall flowing over
your neck and shoulders can be intoxicating. They are also a great
source of entertainment for the younger members of the family.
The LED lights look stunningly beautiful at night and they provide
rainbows of ever-changing colors as they rotate through various
pattern changes, or you can set them to a preferred color.

Paint those pictures. Know your spa inside and out. You may not
always use this vast amount of information in every presentation,
but it's nicer to have it and not need it, than to need it and not
have it.

Spa Presentation Recap

FAB Statements are very powerful and the best method to build
the value of your product. Always confirm the advantage and the
benefit of each feature you mention with your prospect. As your
prospect confirms they see, understand and appreciate the value
of each feature and benefit, their perceived value of your product
increases.

To be the best at your game when presenting a spa, you need to
make your own list of key features and benefits that not only work
in your head, but in your market. What are the five or ten features
you feel you must cover every time you present a spa?

How well do you know your biggest competitors and their product
benefits? What are your competitor's weak spots? Sell against
them in your presentation. Know their top three selling features
and fully expect that your prospect knows them as well and just
might bring them up at some point in your presentation. If you
really want to be the professional, beat them to the punch and
mention the features the prospect may have already seen while

shopping around. It shows you REALLY know your stuff.

You should now have your prospects very excited about owning one of your spas. You will have started to overcome objections based on effective trial closes throughout your presentation and now the only thing separating you from the sale is the money. It is almost time to ask for or "close the sale." Now is when you show you are a professional salesperson. In asking for any sale, you know that certain objections will most likely be revealed. You will be able to confidently overcome objections after reading the next couple chapters. Let's first build some urgency that will motivate your prospect to purchase, today.

Notes

_____

_____

_____

_____

_____

_____

_____

_____

_____

_____

_____

CREATING URGENCY

Creating a Sense of Urgency Will Reduce "Be-Backs" and Close More Sales

A key component in any sales strategy, in addition to a great discovery, establishing solid credibility and a bullet proof product presentation, is to create a sense of urgency for your prospect to buy *now*. The more effective you are at creating urgency, the more sales you will make. Urgency is created in the mind of your prospect by several interesting components: FEAR OF LOSS (this floor model is the last 2008 model we have) and GREED (our half price sale ends tomorrow). Recall the last time you purchased an item the same day you saw it because the deal was too good for you to walk away from. What internal factors motivated you to move forward with the purchase? Was it GREED or a FEAR OF LOSS?

If you don't create some urgency as to why your prospect should act now, right now, why should they? If you don't build sufficient urgency, don't be surprised when your prospect says, "I want to think about it," or "Oh, I'll just buy it later." In the absence of urgency, the prospects' enthusiasm to take advantage of your offering soon fades, or worse yet, they buy the product from a salesman that made the deal too good to walk away from if they bought it today. Believe that your very next prospect, and everyone after that, should buy from you NOW, today. Not tomorrow, not next week or next year. *Now*.

Do you build urgency into your presentation? Don't get me wrong - I am not saying to be like the perceived used car salesman that says, "What do we have to do to get you in this car today?" but to be a sales professional that understands the psychology of the sale and what it takes to help some prospects "over the hump" and make a buying decision on the same day they see your presentation.

Three ways to move your prospect closer to purchasing are to build incredible value during your presentation. Include free options if they purchase today and lastly, discount the price (for a justified reason). In the event you need to throw options or extras in to close the sale, do so, but only after giving that "freebie" a dollar value. If you are including steps and a cover lifter, don't just throw them in - assign a dollar figure to establish their value.

> *"Mr. Prospect, in order to earn your business today, I can offer you a free set of steps worth $399 AND a deluxe cover lifter valued at $499. By making your spa investment with us today, you will receive almost $900 of merchandise for FREE. Does that sound fair to you?"*

If your spa supplier told you all spa stereos you sold today were only $1.99 on the next five spa orders only, do you think you would sell more stereos with your spas? You bet. Why? *Greed* and *fear of loss* in your mind would kick in. Would you be excited about the promotion? Absolutely! You know that you could sell more spas by offering those stereos at half the MSRP all day long and still make a great profit.

Give your prospect a reason to buy now. Everybody wants a good deal. Always have a SPECIAL that is a "great deal" not on the floor – not everybody knows about it. Lower your voice and lean in close to your prospect as if you are sharing a secret.

> *"Mr. Prospect, can I share an exciting opportunity with you?"*

Use this line and your prospect will most likely be leaning in close as well, listening to your every word.

> *"We recently had a promotion on free steps and a free light-ing upgrade. The only problem is the promotion ended two weeks ago. If I could get the same promotion for you today, as we offered during that promotion, would you be inter-ested?"*

Used correctly, urgency will result in your prospects putting self-imposed pressure on themselves to purchase today and help close the sale for you.

If you were an avid golfer and saw a set of high-end golf clubs that you've always wanted, normally priced at $1,500 on SALE for only $499, you would probably seriously consider buying them. If you also learned that there were only two sets left, you probably would buy them and be incredibly proud of your wise investment. If you learned the sale ended today at 5:00 p.m., you know you would buy them and end up calling your golfing buddy to tell him of the incredible sale and that he too must take advantage of this excep-tional deal. Do you see how greed and urgency are used in this example? Can you recall an example in your life when the urgency created to purchase the same day was just too strong and you gave in to it?

Top 10 Statements to Create Urgency

1. "Mr. Prospect, we have some older stock in the back or at the factory *(demo model / limited edition / slight scratch)* that offer some terrific savings. We usually save these deals for our contractors or home builders, if I could offer one of these to you, would you be interested?"

2. "Mr. Prospect, we have a factory promo / store promo that ends tomorrow."

3. "Mr. Prospect, we had a huge factory promotion that ended last week, but we can backdate the paperwork so you can take advantage of the savings from our previous promotion."

4. "Mr. Prospect, the prices you see today are our best prices of the season. Due to a two-day factory promotion, these special prices will only be available until this Friday. Would you like to order one now and take advantage of the savings?"

5. "Mr. Prospect, although we probably will be having another sale next fall, the hot tub you are interested in today is a floor model from last year and is the last one left. As it is a floor model from last year, it is priced far below our current models. Would you like me to reserve it for you and your family so you can take advantage of the savings?"

6. "Mr. Prospect, if you need more time to think about it, I can simply reserve one of our spas for you and your family, for 24 hours, so you can take a little more time to decide without worrying about losing out on this special pricing. All we need to hold your perfect hot tub, and take advantage of this incredible promotion, is a refundable 10 % deposit. Does that sound fair to you?"

7. "Mr. Prospect, I am happy you came into our store today, as we are reaching the end of our 'Fantastic Fall' promotion. Our sale ends tomorrow so your timing is perfect."

8. "Mr. Prospect, this weekend is our 'Super Summer Sale,' and we have three amazing spas that are discounted for this weekend only."

9. "Mr. Prospect, due to excess inventory, we are blowing out three spas to make room for new stock arriving this weekend. Would you like to take advantage of the offer and save hundreds of dollars?"

10. "Mr. Prospect, due to a factory shipping error, we have received one extra floor model. Our spa supplier manufacturers their floor models in large volumes so the production costs are much lower than our regular spas."

When you have a sale or a promotion, explain to your prospect that the special pricing, discount or promotion is from the factory, not from you and your store. If you tell your prospect that you are offering the promotion, they may try to **"be-back"** you and ask for the same deal or discount a week later because they saw *you* offering the promotion. "Oh come on, Mr. Store Owner, you offered me $500 off just last weekend. Why not now?" If the promotion originates from the factory, you are less likely to see the same prospect come back later asking for the same deal you offered last week or last month.

Personally, telling a prospect the sale ends today, in four hours, doesn't fit my presentation style, although it may fit yours perfectly. I much preferred to say to my prospects, "Mr. Prospect, if you are in a position to take advantage of these savings," or "If you are comfortable moving forward with this for your family, the promotion is on until Sunday." I found this far more effective at disarming the prospects' resistance and stress level. The prospect usually ended up saying, "Well, let's just do this now. What difference will a day or two make and we wouldn't have to drive all the way back here again." While on the surface it doesn't look like I tried to close them the same day, I knew if I could deflate their buyer resistance, they were much more likely to purchase from me the same day.

How about this:

"Mr. Prospect, I completely understand how you feel about really needing a few extra days to look around and do your homework. If it were up to me I would certainly extend this weekend's SALE pricing for another week. I think you would agree that wouldn't be fair to those customers that put their

deposits in today to take advantage of the sale pricing. Those owners felt the exact same way you did about wanting to shop around, but what they found was saving hundreds of dollars, if not thousands, by simply putting down a refundable deposit made far more sense that spending several more days shopping around only to discover they were now spending more money and time to receive less. Why don't we go ahead and put your deposit in so you can take advantage of the factory sale prices? Does that sound fair to you?"

Nobody ever wants to feel they have been taken advantage of when buying a product. Everybody wants to be treated fairly and honestly - don't you? A very powerful statement when talking with your prospects is to ask, "Does that sound fair to you?"

One-Time-Only Offers Have a Similar Effect

A one-time offer is just what it sounds like – a special package, price or discount that is offered only once and only for a limited period of time. The key to a successful **one-time** offer is to make it compelling and short- lived. Your prospect will feel an increased urgency to make the purchase.

Make sure that your offer is indeed one-time only. If you repeat an offer too frequently, your potential customers will soon learn that despite all of your advertising and sales pitches to the contrary, there really is no urgency to buy now. They have learned if they wait long enough, another buying opportunity will come along.

A short time frame is important to create urgency. If your sales offer, as good as it may be, is in place for a long period of time, the prospect perceives that there is plenty of time to make a buying decision and may not move forward with their purchase. In other words, the longer he or she has to think about it, the more likely it is that some other distraction will come along and divert attention away from your offer.

About six blocks from my home is a large discount furniture store. Their store windows are covered with very large yellow and black signs screaming, "This Weekend Only Sale," "Huge In-Store Discounts" and "48 Hours Only." To the best of my recollection, that weekend sale has been running for about 18 months. How credible is this offer? What does it tell me about their business practice?

Top 10 Reasons Why your Prospect Should Buy Today

1. Last year's model blow-out
2. Scratch-n-dent floor model
3. Former "wet-test" model
4. Month-end sale to meet quota
5. Factory promotion
6. Incorrect customer order
7. Special draw this weekend, and your purchase provides an entry slip for the draw
8. Big blow-out sale
9. Bulk container purchase
10. Dealer discount certificate

A Free Up-Sell

This tactic can be very effective in creating urgency in your prospects' mind; a free up-sell is simply offering a bonus, upgrade, or other added valuable component to the prospect if they make the purchase right away. These value-added items usually come with an increased price, but if they are able to make the buying decision today, they are included. The key is to make sure your prospect understands that the up-sell offer will not be available after a limited time period.

Up-selling is most effective when the added component is perceived to be a great value, in a limited timeframe or otherwise scarce. This creates the urgency to buy right away or risk losing out on the up-sell offer. Some typical up-sell phrases include "limited quantity available," "while supplies last," or "first five customers only." Regardless of the phrasing you use, the key to success is in creating a sense of scarcity so that the prospect will feel the urgency to buy right away.

To Recap Building Urgency

- Address something painful about not buying your product (sale price today only)

- Make it a limited quantity (this adds scarcity)

- Limit the time to act (promotion ends this weekend)

- Remind your prospect of their hot buttons for purchasing a spa - and what their life will be like without having that pain or problem addressed. Then remind them how they can satisfy their wants, or solve their pain and problems. "Mr. Prospect, you mentioned you have been thinking about owning a spa for years, would you agree there is no better time than now?"

Notes

_____

_____

_____

_____

_____

_____

_____

_____

_____

_____

_____

_____

_____

_____

_____

_____

_____

_____

_____

_____

_____

_____

CLOSING THE SALE

Nothing happens until a sale is made. Closing the sale is merely the continuation and completion of the terrific sales presentation you have already made. It is the logical end to the reason your prospect entered your store. Closing is the final process that brings your prospect to a final decision, be it a yes or a no.

Prepare your Prospect to Buy

It isn't enough to just prepare yourself to ask for the sale; you have to prepare your prospect as well. So how does one do that? By using trial closes. A closing question asks for a final decision, while a trial closing question is one that asks the prospect for an opinion, the answer to which indicates their readiness to buy. This is also known as "taking the prospect's temperature." If your prospect isn't hot enough to buy, don't ask him to buy - it's as simple as that. You need to move your prospect into a receptive mind set so that when asked to purchase, they do.

We looked at trial closes and final closes in the first section; refer back to them as needed. Let's take a closer look at how the sales professional can use different closes to make more sales. The importance of the section can't be emphasized enough - that is why I introduced the concepts well in advance of exploring the sales process so you will be aware to always be listening for the right time to close the sale, be it at the beginning, the middle or at the end of your presentation.. Let's again review this important topic.

Trial Closes

Trial closes are questions that elicit your prospects' opinion.
They are non-threatening questions that ask their opinion and feelings about what you have presented. Typical trial closing questions can build in their directness, as these examples illustrate:

- "How would you feel about owning a floor model and saving some money?"

- "Which of the features do you envision on your hot tub, why?"

- "How do you feel a spa would soothe your aches and pains?"

- "How do you feel about our foot dome? How would that make you feel after a long day of standing?"

- "What would your family feel if this was their new spa?"

- "Which are your favourite options? Why?"

- "How would you feel if we could deliver your new spa for the weekend?"

Your objective is to get your prospects' feelings, opinions and feedback, from the time you meet them until you feel it is time to close the sale. In the absence of trial closing questions, how do you know when it is the right time to close the sale?

After reading this chapter, you will understand that closing the sale, following great trial closing questions, is much easier and far more likely to result in a sale.

The likelihood of your prospect saying yes when you have finally asked for the sale, is far more likely to occur if they have had favourable responses to your trial closes throughout your presentation. Master asking trial closes and your closing ratios will improve substantially.

Trial closes often start with words like *how, what, who* and *would*. See the first section of the book for additional examples of trial closes.

- "How does it sound so far?"
- "What do you like the most of what you have heard?"
- "How does this compare to what you're looking for?"
- "What do you think?"
- "How close do you feel this comes to meeting your needs?"
- "Who do you think would enjoy the spa the most often? Why?"
- "Would this work for you and your family?"

Any question that starts with, "In your opinion..." is a trial close.

"In your opinion, Mr. Prospect, how do you feel this model would suit your family?" is a great trial close.

A positive response to any of these trial closes is usually a sign that you should ask for the order. The key is to have one or two trial closes committed to memory and ready to use.

In general, a strong response to a trial close should lead directly to a closing question. Here are a few trial-close techniques that can instantly turn into a close when the prospect responds in a positive manner.

The first is called the **Recommendation** or **Suggestion** trial close. The idea is for you to act as a resource to your prospect and make a spa recommendation or suggestion that moves the prospect towards a decision in your favour.

> "Mr. Prospect, based on our conversation, I recommend you get the ABC model with the deluxe option package. I really believe this suits your needs for good hydrotherapy and yet still provides you with great family entertainment. What do you think?" or "How does that sound to you?"

A positive response to either of these questions means you're close to making the sale. Ask for the sale.

The **"Would You / If I"** is another technique based on concessions. The basic formula is, "Would you (their commitment), if I (my commitment)?"

> "Mr. Prospect, you mentioned that having the steps, a cover lifter and a year's supply of chemicals was very important to you. Would you buy the spa, if I could get all those items included for you, for free?"

If you are receiving strong buying signals, try the **"What we will do next"** trial close.

> "Mr. Prospect, it sounds like the ABC model is just what you and your family are looking for. What we will do next is get your paperwork completed and your spa ordered. Would that work for you?"

Don't be afraid to use trial closes if you feel that it's the next logical step or after your prospect gives you an especially strong buying signal. Buying signals come in different shapes and sizes, be listening and watching for them.

Top 10 Verbal Buying Signals

1. "This is great!"

2. "Does it come in a different color?"

3. "Do you have others in stock?"

4. "Do you offer financing?"

5. "What's the monthly payment on this one?"

6. "How long is that special promotion on for?"

7. "This would be perfect honey." (No, not to you - to their partner!)

8. "How long does delivery take?"

9. "How long would it take if we ordered a custom model?"

10. "Who is responsible for hooking up the electrical?"

Pay attention not only to the words your prospect uses, but how they say them, their tone and their speed. Do they sound more excited now compared to when you initially started talking with them? Are they more engaged in the dialogue and not just giving short answers? Are they asking more questions? All these are positive buying signals. We communicate not only with our words, but also physically with our bodies as well. In addition to the Top 10 list above, and there are many more than just ten, watch for non-verbal clues and signals. Watch how their body language changes throughout your presentation.

Top 10 Non-Verbal Buying Signals

1. Their arms uncross

2. Prospects lean in towards you more

3. Smiling increases and is more sincere

4. Their hands come out of their pockets

5. They touch the spa more often

6. They start inspecting the spa more closely

7. They loosen clothing or take off a jacket

8. They are more physically animated

9. Eye contact is increased

10. Their body is square towards you

If you have the time and the interest, the study of body language is fascinating. Go online and do a quick search on the topic of body language. There are many free articles for you to read and learn from. If it looks like an area of study you would like to explore, spend $20 and buy a book - you won't regret it.

Failure to Use Trial Closes

Three primary reasons why salespeople aren't comfortable using trial closes:

1. They are not finished selling (actually *telling*) and don't want their pitch interrupted by something as mundane as getting the sale.

2. They confuse a trial close with the *final close* and force the prospect to make a final decision instead of asking for an opinion; this often results in "I need to think about it."

3. They simply aren't prepared to use them.

Some salespeople don't know how to use trial closes effectively.

Because trial closes are so non-threatening, they can be used early in the presentation and as often as you feel the need to take the prospect's temperature and solicit their feedback.

Trial Close Responses

When you ask your prospect, "Do you feel this is what you've been looking for?" and they respond with, "Absolutely! I've been looking for something like this for a long time. It looks great!" you should consider that a hot response and go for a close by asking for the business.

What if your prospect responded to your trial close with, "It's sort of what I'm looking for" or "I'm just not sure" or some other luke-warm response? In this situation, going for a close is risky at best and a better approach is to continue selling by presenting additional benefits and reasons for the prospect to buy and then use another trial close to test the waters again.

While getting a completely stone-cold response to a trial close is unusual, it can and does happen. For example, what should you do if you ask the question, "How do you feel this meets your needs in what you're looking for?" and the response is, "It doesn't" I think it goes without saying that this should be considered a cold response. If you have a death wish, you can keep on selling and continue to pile on additional benefits and reasons to buy in the hopes of turning the situation around. All you will do is annoy your prospect. He has just told you flat out that your presentation is off the mark and any continued attempts to go in the same direction are only going to result in you digging an even deeper hole for yourself. Don't be afraid to ask for another salesperson to look after them if you feel you have not connected with them. Sometimes we just don't mesh with the person in front of us. It is not a reflection of you or them, sometimes it just happens. If you realize that from the first hello your personalities clashed, doesn't it make more sense to ask another salesperson to take over the presentation? Explain to your prospect that you were just getting ready to return a telephone call or enter a meeting and if they wouldn't mind, one of the other sales staff would gladly address their questions.

"Mr. Prospect, I really must apologize, I didn't realize I have a meeting starting in a few minutes. Would you be offended if I had another member of our staff continue explaining our products?"

If you are feeling a tension between you and the prospect, they are feeling it as well. Ask another staff member to step in, introduce your prospects and take a moment to review what you have discussed and where you are in your presentation, and then disappear for 10 or 15 minutes. I have had several occasions where "flipping" the prospect resulted in a colleague making the sale and the prospects coming up to me after and thanking me for my time. Selling is a team exercise in these unique situations.

What should you do if you are getting icy cold responses to your trial closes? Immediately stop selling and re-qualify your prospect to find out what went wrong. Why are you continuing to mention product benefits that are completely missing the target? Did you misunderstand something the prospect told you earlier? Did you not build enough rapport or establish credibility? Has something changed that you didn't pick up? Whatever it is, find out what is going on before continuing to sell.

Can you answer these questions in regards to your prospects' needs:

Top 10 Questions That Address Your Prospects' Needs

1. Agreed on a place to put it?
2. Agreed to a model?

3. Agreed to a color?

4. Agreed to siding options?

5. Agreed to specific features and options?

6. Agreed to a time frame?

7. Discussed how they will pay for it?

8. Decided when the first backyard spa party will be held?

9. Decided when the spa should be delivered?

10. Did you address any major concerns that may prevent the sale?

If the answers are yes, it is time to close the sale.

Closing the Sale Recap

A prospect will buy from you if:

- They feel BETTER about buying a hot tub *after* speaking to you, than they did *before* speaking to you.

- You have made a connection and made a friend.

- They trust you. (If they don't buy the messenger, they won't buy the message.)

Did you help them answer the following questions:

- Do I need this spa?

- Is this the right spa for me?

- Is this the right company to buy it from?

- Is this the right person to buy it from?

- Is this the right time to buy it?

- Is this the right price for the value?

Opportunities to close:

- In your greeting
- During your credibility building
- During your discovery
- While giving your product presentation
- While handling objections
- During the close
- After the sale

The opportunities to close at the right time are endless. Do you know the major reason why prospects don't buy? They were never asked! That's right - no one asked them for the business. Never let a prospect leave your showroom without asking them to purchase.

Strange as it seems, salespeople use all their superior selling skills to get in front of a prospect, qualify them, establish huge credibility, uncover the prospects' needs, present their products and then they stand back and wait for the prospect to figure out how to complete the sale instead of taking the final step of helping them make the purchase.

There are three main reasons why salespeople don't ask for the business:

1. They don't know what to do.
2. They don't know how to do it.
3. They don't want to do it.

Let's take a look at the last reason. We all know why salespeople don't want to ask for the order. It's the word "NO." Apparently, a "NO" is 10-feet tall and made of solid concrete. When a "NO" falls on a salesperson, it crushes him or her to death. I've never personally known a salesperson to die from getting a "NO." On the other hand, I have known a few who've nearly suffered a heart attack from receiving a "Yes" they weren't expecting! It seems many salespeople would rather hear, "I need to think about it" than a flat out "NO."

Sensitive Egos

The egos of salespeople are far more sensitive than most people will ever realize; we are easily bruised. We don't like the feeling of rejection that comes with hearing the word no. Contrary to popular belief, our egos really are very tender and fragile. When a prospect rejects our fabulous offer, we're often crushed. After three crushes, we become demoralized, and who needs that? So, as the theory goes, we try to keep our egos intact by avoiding the "noes," and we avoid "noes" by not asking for the order.

If you are to continue succeeding in the sales game, you must keep in mind that you've got nothing to lose by attempting to close the sale. You didn't have the business before the attempt and you may not have the business after. But one thing is for sure — you'll be one "no" closer to getting a "yes," if you just have the courage to ask.

Many salespeople will say they know exactly how to close the sale but, when push comes to shove, they are more talk than action.

Find What Works

Choose a couple of closing techniques that suit your style and that you feel comfortable using. Now write the actual words you intend to use on a 3" x 5" card. Keep this card on the dashboard of your car, on your fridge, wherever you will see it and practice the words until you have them committed to memory.

Tell yourself that you owe it to your prospects, your company, and to yourself to at least attempt a close at the appropriate time. How does this logic sound to you? There are two ways to avoid getting the dreaded no at the end of your presentation. The easiest way is to simply not ask for the sale. Unfortunately, too many salespeople use this approach and hope the prospect will just step and ask to buy. This is probably not the best technique. The other option is to continually test the waters using trial closes with your prospect.

As you continue to practice your trial closes, and see how successful they really are, you will gain increased confidence and find that you receive far more "yeses" than "noes." In your opinion, isn't this how it really should be? Do you know what the very best close is in any business offering any product? It is an exciting and enthusiastic presentation that fosters desire.

Final Closing Questions

This Is It - Time To Ask For The Business

In asking these final closing questions, a lot will depend on your confidence to ask for the sale. Below are many powerful closing questions. These are generally safer to use if you are not comfortable directly asking for the sale outright. As you gain more confidence, your closings will shift from questions to more assumptive statements. In the examples below, a more assumptive statement, which takes far more confidence to use, follows each closing question and you must absolutely assume your prospect will purchase.

Your prospect can smell fear and if you are not comfortable asking for the business, they will see right through you. You will notice with the first closing question or request to move forward, that the prospect has the option of saying "NO" and stopping you in your tracks. With the more assumptive close, if your prospect wants to stop you, they have to actively engage you and say they are not interested. In this case, you would have a lot more directions to go than just hearing a "NO." Does that make sense to you?

Of course, your heart will beat faster and your palms will be far sweatier if you are not used to using assumptive closes. This may be brand new for you, especially if you are not initially confident in asking for the sale. This anxiety is completely normal and will pass with practice. No salesperson has ever died from asking for the sale, at least none that I am aware of. The examples below have two distinct styles of asking for the sale. The first is less assumptive, the second example is very assumptive; choose the style you are most comfortable using as they must suit your personality and presentation style.

It is very important after you ask a closing question to shut up. Sorry if I seem blunt, but you really need to just shut up and hear your prospects' reply in full. Here is when time will drag on and a moment will seem like eternity, but you must be silent and wait for your prospects' response, as your next comment will depend entirely on their response.

Transition from Presentation to Close

Top 10 Closing Questions and Assumptive Closes

1. "Would you like to go ahead with this?"

2. "Let's go ahead with this."

3. "We can start the process today with a credit card if you'd like."

4. "All I need is your credit card to start the process. Who will get the air miles?"

5. "We can deliver it to you by the weekend if you'd like."

6. "It will be delivered to your house on Saturday afternoon."

7. "Should I grab an invoice so you can get started enjoying your new hot tub as soon as possible?"

8. "I'll grab an invoice so you can get started enjoying your new hot tub as soon as possible."

9. "It'll take a few weeks to manufacture and ship your new spa so if you're comfortable in moving forward, we should start the paperwork now."

10. "It'll take a few weeks to manufacture and ship your new spa so let's get the paperwork started now."

Top 10 Strong Closing Statements

1. "Let's get this off your plate and wrap up the paperwork."

2. "Let's wrap this up so you can get on to your other priorities."

3. "It seems we are in agreement. I'll grab the order form."

4. "It looks like you've made up your mind to get a spa for your family."

5. "It sounds like you don't have any more questions. Let's get the paperwork started."

6. "Mr. Prospect, you have worked very hard all your life. You have earned this."

7. "Mr. Prospect, it is time for those four magic words, 'Marco, we'll take it.'"

8. "Mr. Prospect, this is the part of my presentation where you say, 'YES'."

9. "Mr. Prospect, if you are finished beating me up, I'll grab your paperwork."

10. "Mr. Prospect, all we need now are a couple of signatures."

My Two Personal Favourite Closes

Please keep in mind if any of you have seen me selling, I have a very playful and interactive presentation based on a very strong rapport and humour -- a lot of humour. I believe buying a hot tub should be fun for both you and your prospects.

Always sit your prospect down before presenting any prices; it is far harder for them to get up and leave when you are all sitting down together at a table. I would try to ask these two favourite closes before I presented any written prices. Their reaction to these two closes often indicated how close I was to making the sale or if I needed to re-address something before I showed the numbers.

1. "Mr. Prospect, before I show how affordable your new spa is, let me ask you a question. If the spa you liked so much was FREE, would you want it? Yes, I hear that a lot. If it was $1,000,000, chances are the answer would be NO, is that correct? Is it fair to say that somewhere between FREE and $1,000,000 is a number that will work for you and your budget today?"

2. "Mr. Prospect, purchases such as this usually come down to three things: like, use and affordability. Is it fair to say you like what you saw today? If you were to win this stunning spa in a contest, I am guessing you wouldn't have to think about it and you would probably use it. Would that be correct? Well, that only leaves the 'A' word, affordability. We don't want to see you and your family eating macaroni

and cheese for the next five years, so if we can make this completely affordable to you, is this something you would do today for your family?"

In the mind of the prospect, the various sample closes I have listed are much easier questions to absorb, acknowledge and accept than, "Do you want to buy it?" and "How will you pay for this?" Notice most of the sample closes don't even ask the prospect for their money. The prospect knows they will have to use their money, but in a gentle way, we are not directly asking them for their money. This wording works to nullify the natural defense mechanism we all have, right when we are about to part with our hard- earned cash.

Now that you have seen examples of various closes, copy the format and apply it to your own situation. Take your new closes into the bathroom or in front of any mirror and practice pitching with them. Observe your body language when you ask for the close. Make sure you are direct but not confrontational, stern but nonchalant, and make eye contact. Blankly staring at the numbers on the paper will only spook your prospect as they pick up on your lack of confidence. You are helping them realize a dream, not just selling them a product.

Your closing statements need to roll off your tongue as if you have done this hundreds of times and everyone is buying.

Now that you have "done the dead" and asked for the sale, there are only two possible outcomes: either they purchased or they did not. In the likely event they purchased, CONGRATULATIONS, you have earned it. Now don't forget a great follow-up with your newest owner and you have hit a home run out of the park. After your newest customers have left your store, get back on the telephone and follow-up on those prospects you haven't closed yet.

In the event your prospect didn't immediately say yes to your offer, they will have had voiced objections. Objections are those minor little roadblocks, if you see them as minor, which stand between you and your prospect completing the sale. Overcoming objections is where the true sales professional really brings their "A" game.

There is no magic formula in closing. It is often said closing is 70 percent attitude, 20 percent technique and 10 percent skill. Prepare yourself, prepare the prospect, and do the deed. You owe it to your prospect, to your company, and most important of all, you owe it to yourself to ask for the sale.

Notes

_____

_____

_____

_____

_____

_____

_____

_____

Overcoming Objections

After reading this chapter you will have a better understanding of what objections really are, why they occur and the reasons they are being made. You will have all the tools necessary to overcome them and close more sales. How many sales do you think are lost because of a lack of knowledge or the tools to overcome your prospects' objections? Sadly, there are many. Most sales are won or lost at the objection stage!

The Top 10 Guaranteed Ways to Instantly Blow the Sale When Dealing With Objections or "How Not to Build Rapport With Your Prospects"

1. Argue with them
2. Guess at your answers, or worse yet, lie
3. Blame others for issues
4. Tell your prospect flat out they are wrong
5. Prove them wrong, especially in front of others
6. Contradict your prospect
7. Verbally attack them and their beliefs
8. Insult them
9. Dwell too long on objections
10. Ignore their objections

Hopefully you had a laugh when reading my Top 10 list, but sadly they are all based on real attempts to unsuccessfully address objections I have heard during sales presentations. I am sure you can appreciate the names of the offenders and the specific details have been deliberately omitted, but you all know who you are!

Building Rapport

As a sales professional, dealing with objections is a part of our business that will never go away. Overcoming objections is a very necessary and valuable component of the sales process.

You have two choices when it comes to addressing objections: either fully understand what they are, what they really mean and learn to overcome them or get out of sales because you won't be selling for long if you can't overcome objections. As I stated before, every sales professional knows all sales are won or lost at the objections stage. How well you overcome objections is directly related to how successful you were in building a strong rapport with your prospect and the effort you have put in to learning how to understand and overcome them. In the absence of a strong rapport, overcoming objections will be difficult, if not impossible. Having built a strong rapport, you will be far more successful in overcoming objections as you have already had a mutual exchange of thoughts and ideas with your prospect. In the absence of strong rapport, you will be seen as a pushy salesperson only interested in selling a product.

Perception

Remember we discussed perception earlier? This is where your perception of what objections really mean to you is incredibly important. Just what goes through your mind when you hear an objection? Is it that you have lost the sale? Is an objection this 10-

foot high wall of bricks, steel and pointy bits that will come crash-
ing down on you if your prospect says no? Will it crush your ego
and ruin the rest of your day? Will you huddle with the other sales
staff in the coffee room and complain how bad the prospects are
or how bad the economy is, all because you couldn't handle an
objection? How you perceive and handle objections is entirely up
to you.

This chapter will provide you with the techniques and strategies to
overcome objections.

It is up to you to learn, practice and apply these skills.
A great way to have the world's shortest sales career is to shy
away from overcoming objections. Objections are the mediocre
salespersons' worst nightmare, because it requires them to:

- Know their product inside and out.

- Have a compelling answer for any objection.

- Face the fear of rejection from the prospect when addressing their objections.

Most people think they can easily and effectively handle objections.
The reality is overcoming objections is the crucial component of
sales where most salespeople have the most difficulty. If you feel
you are great with overcoming objections, then you should score
quite well on the self-quizzes in this chapter. If you are new to
sales, or a seasoned professional who feels overcoming objections
is an area where you could improve, LEARN THIS CHAPTER!
Read and re-read this valuable information until you are completely comfortable overcoming any objection. In addition to having a handful of rebuttals, (of course, it is a given you will already
have some great objection rebuttals) focus on understanding your
prospects' thinking behind the objection, as it is also crucial to your
success in closing more sales and increasing your income.

A friendly reminder: most sales are won or lost at the objection stage!

Objections often result when your prospect has these thoughts:

- No perceived value in spa ownership

- No trust in you, your store or your products

- No perceived urgency in purchasing the spa

- Perception of the superiority of a competitor's offering

- A lack of funds to purchase your offering

- "It's safer to do nothing" perception or a fear of making any commitment

Always keep these concerns in the back of your mind when you hear your prospects' objections. These concerns are often expressed as "We need to think about it." For a more detailed understanding of this important section, see the sample objections that follow at the end of the chapter.

Handling Objections

- How well do you handle objections?

- Are you just mediocre in your reply, good, or really great at it?

- Do you have a method for understanding and handling any objection?

- Do you find yourself mumbling and fumbling or worse yet, do you sit there dumbfounded in front of your prospect, not knowing what to say?

- Do you find yourself completely changing the subject hoping your prospect won't notice?

- Do you remember great responses only AFTER your prospect has left your store?

If these sound familiar, don't feel bad, as it has happened to EVERY sales professional on the planet at one time or another in their career. Until you understand what motivates the objection and discover how to overcome objections effectively, your success in sales will be limited. Learn from the experience of unanswered objections. Write them down and address them after the prospect leaves your store. Be prepared to overcome them *the very next time* you hear them.

Overcoming objections is crucial for successful selling, no matter what product or service you are selling. Only when you master the skills and gain the confidence to ask your prospect the right questions to fully understand and counter their objections, will you be far closer to closing the sale. Ask questions that will address common objections and commit your prospect to purchase. The person asking the questions is the person in control and being in control is the key to getting the sale.

Facing your Fears

Do not be afraid of objections - objections are a good thing! Your prospect brings them up because they are interested in buying your products, but need direction. Think of it this way: if they were not really interested in purchasing your products or services, wouldn't they just ask for a brochure and leave your store? If they are still standing in front of you after voicing their concerns or objections, they WANT to be there. SELL THEM! Sadly, I have seen far too many salespeople think addressing objections means they will morph into the stereotypical image of the used car salesman (my sincerest apologies to all the true car sales professionals in the world), in their color-contrasting plaid suits, beating and intimidating their prospect into purchasing.

There is a world of difference between being pushy and truly understanding the prospects' concerns and successfully overcoming them. If you have been successful in building a strong rapport with your prospect, it is okay to ask questions to better determine the nature of their objections. Recall we *did* ask for and *receive* the prospects' permission to ask questions in the beginning of the presentation. Through your prospects' objections, they are sharing with you exactly what their wants and needs really are that you have not yet addressed to their satisfaction. Only by uncovering their real objections and dealing with them immediately will you be in a position to sell to your prospect. Unaddressed or unknown objections have an amazing way of coming back later to haunt you when you least expect it.

Opportunity is Knocking – Are You Listening?

Think of your prospects' objections as questions and not really objections. They are a way for them to justify their investment in you and your products. Rarely does anyone make a purchase of a "high-ticket" item without asking questions first, especially internal questions such as, "Am I making the right choice?" or "Am I getting good value for my money?" Recall a time you were considering making a "high-ticket" investment or purchase. Did you just listen to the sales presentation and purchase outright or did you ask questions and express areas of concern that needed to be addressed before you made the purchase?

Were your prospects merely asking a question, asking for clarity on certain points or truly not interested in your product or services and blowing you off with a "fluffy" objection? Try to see overcoming objections as a necessary process that is moving you one step closer to closing the sale. With practice, your confidence will increase and you will learn how to use your prospects' objections as closing tools; with practice, you will be able to use their objections as the reasons they *should* purchase your products or services.

For the most part, the successful sales professional sees objections as positive signs (just a question or two that needs to be effectively addressed before completing the sale). Objections are multi-faceted opportunities for you to focus on areas or issues that you may have unknowingly omitted during your presentation.

How you handle yourself in addressing objections crucial. What practice exercises do you go through to improve your objection handling skills? Do you make a conscious effort to learn how to overcome objections or do you just hope and pray they will magically go away and never come up again? Since your prospects are interested in buying, you need to make sure that your tone and your demeanor reflect the positive attributes of their objections when they bring them up. Do not become discouraged or defensive about your presentation, product or your company. Your prospects are interested in buying from you; they are standing in front of you. They simply need more clarification or understanding to move forward with their purchase.

Understanding the Secret

The secret in overcoming objections lies in understanding exactly what they want to know more about and why. Objections come in many forms - you must decipher exactly what it is that they are really asking or saying and what it is they are truly concerned about and why. You need to understand the objection to overcome it. You must understand whether or not their objection is just a question or is it really an objection which could be a serious road block preventing you from moving forward with the sale.

1. Discovering the Truth

The first objection you receive may not always be the real reason they are not moving forward with their investment in your product; it may be a smoke screen to cover their real objection. "I need to think about it" can easily be a smoke screen for "I can't afford it but I can't tell you my finances are really bad." (This can be a saving face gesture.)

Let's look at an example:

P = *Prospect,* S = *Salesperson*

P: "We need to go home and think about it."

S: "Do you mind if I ask you what is the reason you are making the decision to not move forward today?"

At this point the prospect may share the reason for their objection.

S: "Is that the only reason?"

P: "Yes."

S: "Then if we can (eliminate the objection), would you move forward with this for your family today?"

P: "Yes."

2. Clearing the Fluff and the Smokescreen

S: "Then if we can (eliminate the objection), would you move forward with this for your family today?"

P: "No."

S: "It sounds like there must be another concern – what might that be?"

P: "The spa is more than we had budgeted for."

S: "Other than the affordability, is there any other concern?"

P: "No."

S: "So if I understand you correctly, if we can find a spa that meets your needs and fits into your budget, you will be able to move forward with us today?"

P: "Yes."

S: "What budget range did you have in mind?"

More often than not, the real objection is usually price-related and your prospects' ability to justify the investment in their minds. How do I know that? If your spas were half price, you would likely be sold out and there would be a line-up of people around the block wanting your products. Does that make sense? If we eliminate the price objection, you will almost always have a sale. It is up you, the sales professional, to clear all the fluff and smoke away and get to the real objection. If you feel you are getting many unrealistic objections, you must work to narrow down your prospects' objections and eliminate the false ones until finally there is only the true one left. If you are unsuccessful in finding *and* overcoming the true objection, you will be left wondering what happened and why you lost the sale. Overcome the true objection, and you should have a sale.

I recall hosting a sales training seminar in a small town in Alberta, Canada, a few years ago. The sales staff and I had spent half the day focusing on improving listening skills and successfully overcoming objections, as these were the areas they felt they needed to improve on. A prospect had walked into the store asking questions about spa ownership. One of the sales staff stepped up to address the prospects' needs and give a presentation. Let's call her Lorie.

Lorie gave a great presentation, asking terrific open-ended questions and trial closes throughout her presentation. When time came to close the sale, Lorie was met with the standard objection, "I have to think about it." As she was very uncomfortable in overcoming objections and didn't want to be seen as "the pushy salesperson," she fell back to her safety position and offered the prospect a nice shiny brochure and an invitation for him to come back to the store when he was ready to purchase. She even went so far as to suggest he shop around at their competitors, hoping he would be-back. (Yes, this is a true story.)

Do you see where this is headed? I saw this as an ideal time to step up and hopefully teach through example of how to overcome the objection. I respectfully introduced myself to the gentleman and explained that I was the sales trainer for the hot tub manufacturer and that I was in the store to help the staff improve their presentation skills. I politely asked if I could ask him a few questions. "What would you like to know?" was the reply.

I asked what he thought of Lorie's presentation that he had just heard, and whether there were any particular areas of concern that he had to "think about." His reply was very interesting and not soon forgotten. "Marco, I don't know if it will fit." Yes, you read that correctly - he was unsure if the spa would fit. I spent a couple of minutes building rapport and asked a few more questions based on his concerns. He explained that he and his wife had just built a new deck off the back of the house and his concern was whether or not the spa he liked so much would fit.

I replied, "So if I understand you correctly, the spa you like (model ABC) is perfect for you and your family and the only concern you have is whether it will fit on your new deck? Do I have that correct?" His reply was "YES". "Of course, that is a very good concern. Well, if your only concern is the spa fitting on your new deck, why don't we just go around to your house right now and see if it fits?"

He thought that was a great idea and appreciated the personal visit to his house so he could proudly show off the beautiful deck he had just built. I suggested that in the interest of saving him time, it would make more sense to put the paperwork together now while he was in the store. A simple 20% deposit was all that would be required to hold the floor model he wanted so it wouldn't be sold to another family. The site inspection and sale went through without a hitch. With many handshakes and big smiles, he thanked us for our time and personal attention.

Don't we all wish sales were that easy? The town he lived in had at least six competitors that certainly would have gladly stepped up and made the sale if we had not made the effort to understand his concerns and the resulting "objection." Lorie realized that asking questions to address concerns wasn't a bad thing - just the opposite. Being a "pushy" sales professional is not what you should be striving for. Being the very best sales professional you can be is the goal. Lorie, if you are reading this, I thank you for the experience and opportunity to work with you.

Do You "Wing It" or "Can't Wait to Hear What I'm Going to Say Today"

A good salesperson shouldn't randomly "wing" their responses to objections. While on the surface a great salesperson's responses look effortless, they only look effortless due to study, understanding and practice. *A lot of practice.* The professional salesperson anticipates what their prospects might say and is prepared to respond accordingly.

Take a moment to write down the five most common objections you get from your prospects. Does it make sense to know ahead of time the common objections you receive time and again and NOT have a way to reply or respond to them?

1)_____

2)_____

3)_____

4)_____

5)_____

Would you not agree it is a great idea to practice your responses to the five objections you receive the most often? Practice with your store colleagues and brainstorm different ideas to overcome these common objections.

Do you really want to be a great sales professional and increase your closing average and your paycheck?

It is entirely up to you. Learning how to overcome objections is one of the fundamental keys of selling. What do you think would happen if you addressed and overcame those common objections *during* your presentation? One of the best sayings a mentor of mine shared with me was, "Bash the snake's head, before it rises." If you already know you are going to get standard objections that are common to your business, you need to have your responses memorized and well rehearsed ahead of hearing those objections. In mentioning and overcoming common objections *during* your presentation, you will completely disarm your prospect, look like the sales professional you are, and put your prospect in a more positive and receptive frame of mind for purchasing your product because you appear to be the expert.

When Is the Right Time?

There are four different times to handle your prospects objections:

1. Before they occur

2. When they occur

3. Later on

4. Never

Ideally, *before* they occur is the best time!

Start eliminating future objections during your presentation, before they are brought up. Can you give an example of this? You know the objection of "We need to think about it" will often come up. Pepper your dialogue with comments that address this objection following a positive response to a feature and benefit. Try this reply after one of those "Wow" replies.

"You really didn't have to think about that now, did you?"

With the benefits they strongly acknowledge, ask, "You really didn't have to think about that one either did you?" Obviously, don't use this reply every time with every benefit, mix it up.

Share third party stories during your presentation.

"Mr. Prospect, I am reminded of a couple of terrific customers of mine, Dan and his lovely wife, Deb. They purchased one of our spas a few years back and what really surprised me is that Dan said he had been thinking about this for almost eight years. I had conducted a good discovery and learned Dan was a carpet layer. If you are not familiar with this particular profession, you need only remember one fact: carpet layers' hands and knees are horribly beat up. A carpet layers' primary tool is a carpet kicker. Dan explained this is a metal rod about two feet long, with sharp teeth on

one end and a four square inch 'pad' with no more than two inches of padding on the other end. To use it is simple: place the end with the teeth on the carpet facing the wall and the other end towards yourself. While balanced on just your hands and knees, you lift one knee off the ground and then slam that knee as hard as you can against the small tiny pad; this gradually stretches the carpet towards the wall. Dan said he had slammed his knee against the knee kicker hundreds of times everyday, for years. A carpet layers' knees will usually look like two under inflated volleyballs; this is not an exaggeration. Dan shared with me that each year he looked around, he always told the salesperson, "I need to think about it." After he left the store, he thought about it…for 8 years, until he met me.

"Dan and Deb decided to 'take the plunge' and invest in a spa. Money was tight for them so they felt they could only purchase a mid-priced spa. They were in the process of building a deck and wouldn't need the spa for a couple of months; however, they made the purchase early to take advantage of the sale pricing we were having that weekend. The three of us had hit it off extremely well and they often popped into the store to grab a coffee with me and have a visit.

"Well, the big day finally arrived. We delivered their spa in the morning and it was up and running that same night. Done deal, right? To my absolute horror, the very next day, both Dan and Deb walked back in to the store with very flat and sombre expressions, explained I was to take the spa back as they didn't want it. You can't even begin to imagine how I felt; my heart sank. I thought we had started to become friends through all their store visits and this was the last thing I ever expected to happen."

"With a sleight stutter in my voice, I asked what had happened. "Did something break?" I will never ever forget Dan's *reply. "Marco, (a big grin started to stretch across his face), we used the spa last night for an hour and then went off to bed. That was the very best sleep I have ever had in my entire life." Remember, he had originally purchased one of our more 'cost-conscious' spas. After that one great night of sleep he decided he wanted to trade his spa back in and purchase our biggest and baddest spa with all the bells, whistles and jets that we could put into it. This easily more than doubled the initial price he paid for the 'cost-conscious' spa. He quickly realized if he slept better, he felt healthier and was much happier. He felt it would be much easier for him to get through his painful days of kicking carpets, knowing a relaxing soak in his hot tub would complete his day. Based on these benefits, he now easily justified the increased cost associated with owning the best spa we had."*

"He called me the next day to report, "Marco that was the second best sleep I have ever had. I can't believe I waited eight years to do this. I should have purchased a hot tub years ago." This is a true story and I had many referrals from Dan and his colleagues in the carpet business."

I would often share this "third party story" with prospects that "wanted to think about it." I would gently remind them not to be like Dan and Deb and "think about it" for years. "Mr. Prospect, you now understand how owning a spa will help you feel better and you said you wanted to feel better, so let me ask you a question. When is a good time to start to feeling better - now or in another eight years?"

Snake Bashing 101

Deflate objections *before* your prospect has a chance to bring them up.

> *"Mr. Prospect, when some of our customers first visit us, they are surprised to see only a few models in the $5,995 to $6,995 price range, like many box stores offer. When they see the features that are available in the $6,995 to $11,995 range, they realize that the cheaper spas they saw at the local box store are missing many of the 'must have' features."*

If you want to look like a sales professional and bring up common objections before your prospect does, try a few of these phrases. Fill in the examples with the common objections you hear, and practice overcoming them ahead of time, during your presentation.

- "You are probably thinking…"
- "You might be asking yourself…"
- "You might be wondering…"
- "If you're concerned about…"
- "A question I often hear at this point in our conversation is…"

Now the fun part, let's explore how to successfully overcome objections.

Basic Rules for Overcoming Sales Objections

Let's review the basic "overcoming objection" strategies before we get into more specific techniques.

Top 10 Basic Strategies to Overcoming Objections

1. Stay calm, relaxed and focused as you WILL receive objections; sometimes many, sometimes only a few, but you will get them. Your prospect may be watching closely to see what your reaction is to their comments.

2. Compliment your prospect on bringing up a terrific point. They will appreciate your professional opinion of their concerns.

3. Agree with the prospect about something. This will serve to cushion and soften the objection. Add something that they can't disagree with regarding their objection. It makes them feel as if you understand their objection.

4. **Ask questions** to uncover the real reason for the objection by asking **what** and **why** questions. The more open-ended questions you ask, the more information you will glean.

5. Listen with sincere interest, hear your prospect out and NEVER interrupt, as tempting as it may be to do so. Your prospects will often expose their real reasons for not buying. They will often provide you with new information that will help you better understand their concerns.

6. Avoid generalities when answering objections. Your prospect has raised a concern; deal with it head-on. Avoid long-winded answers to objections; if you spend a long time focusing on your reply, it will only reinforce in your prospects' mind their objection may truly be an area of concern. Address the objection clearly and concisely and then return to your sales presentation. Ask your prospect if that addresses their concern. "Does that make sense to you?" "Did that explain it?"

7. Even if you already have a response, count to three BE-

FORE you speak, as that shows you are really thinking about their concerns and not just rattling off a standard response. Restate their objection in your own words. This shows your prospect you were truly listening and genuinely trying to address their concerns, not just sell them your products. You have the added benefit of restating the objection in a more favourable way. "So if I understand you correctly…"

8. All people, not just in sales but also in life, are far more inclined to listen to you after they know you have listened to them. Always remember the Top 10 list on how to lose a sale covered at the beginning of this chapter. Tuck this information away in the back of your brain and strive to do just the opposite.

9. Never argue with your prospect. This can't be said enough. Oftentimes you will be right and your prospect will be wrong. Winning the argument will only ensure that you'll lose the sale.

10. Don't ever lie or try to guess at an answer. Admit you don't know and promise to find the correct answer before they leave, and find it. It proves your honesty and integrity to your prospect. If you guess or lie, and are wrong or caught in the lie, you will have just lost all the credibility and trust you have built up. It might just cost you the sale.

Yes, I said it before, and will continue to repeat myself: anticipate and prevent objections before they are raised.

I recall working with a very nice older couple some years back when I worked in retail spa sales. They were considering purchasing a new spa. I believed my presentation was first rate and I thought all that was needed to complete the sale was a couple of signatures. It turned out they were quite religious and talked about needing to go to church and pray before making their purchase.

Wow, I don't think I have ever had THAT objection before; but I had to completely respect their religious beliefs.

Take a moment and ask yourself how you would proceed if this couple was in front of you and voiced that objection. Rather than ignore their concern or just hope it would go away, I quickly realized the only direction I could take would be to better understand their objection. Politely, (having built up a terrific rapport) I asked them about why it was so important that they needed to pray. "God guides us in everything we do," they replied. I asked them if they thought it was a coincidence they were standing in front of me today. They bought their dream spa.

Advanced Rules for Overcoming Objections

'Overcoming objections' is a simple four-step process:

1. Acknowledge the Objection

To have any chance of overcoming your prospects' objections, remember you must first have put the effort into building a strong rapport throughout your presentation. (Yes, I will endeavor to repeat this point many more times through out the book.) In responding to any objection, always acknowledge your prospects' concerns with an affirmation so they feel acknowledged for their objections.

Top 10 Objection Acknowledgments Statements

1. "Mr. Prospect, I am really glad you brought that up."

2. "Mr. Prospect, that is a great question."

3. "Mr. Prospect, you have obviously been listening very closely and I appreciate that."

4. "Mr. Prospect, I often hear the same intelligent concerns that you are voicing right now."

5. "Mr. Prospect, good point. You mean that's the only reason you're not buying?"

6. "Mr. Prospect, that is a very interesting point."

7. "Mr. Prospect, that is a very legitimate concern."

8. "Mr. Prospect, great question."

9. "Mr. Prospect, thank you for sharing that with me."

10. "Mr. Prospect, excellent comment, I'm very glad you brought that up."

2. Isolate, Indentify and Rephrase the Objection

When you take the time to listen and rephrase the objection, your prospect knows that you are paying attention to them. Rephrasing clarifies the objection to avoid any misunderstandings. It also gives you a moment to gather your thoughts. By rephrasing to better identify their real issues, you can lighten their concerns, or probe for more information.

Top 10 Objection Isolation, Identification and Rephrase Statements, with a Couple of Extras

1. "Mr. Prospect, would you mind explaining why you feel that way?"

2. "Mr. Prospect, don't you really mean..."

3. "Mr. Prospect, so you're telling me..."

4. "Mr. Prospect, do I understand you to mean that..."

5. "Mr. Prospect, that is a very interesting point. Do you mind helping me understand why you feel that way?"

6. "Mr. Prospect, I can appreciate that, so what you are saying is..."

7. "Mr. Prospect, obviously you have a good reason for saying that. Do you mind if I ask what it is?" "Just supposing (we can meet the condition), then do you feel you could proceed?"

8. "So if I understand you correctly..."

9. "So what I am hearing is..."

10. "So what you really mean is...?"

11. "Is that the only concern you have?"

12. "Is this the only issue that is preventing us from moving forward today?"

13. "Other than that, is there anything else preventing you from moving forward?"

14. "Other than (the objection), is that your only concern?"

3. Overcome the Objection

You should now have a much better understanding of their objection and why it is important to them. In order to address and overcome their objection, you may have to backtrack or repeat parts of your presentation to more fully explain a feature or a policy to their satisfaction or understanding. In addressing ANY objection, you need to confirm your reply to their objection has been not only received, but also understood. Don't overcome an objection and leave it hanging out there; confirm it hit the mark.

Top 10 Confirmations You Have Successfully Addressed Their Objection:

1. "Now that solves the problem, doesn't it?"

2. "When you think of it that way, how do you feel about this spa now?"

3. "I guess we've made that clear now, haven't we?"

4. "Does that make sense now?"

5. "Are you comfortable that we have addressed that to your satisfaction?"

6. "That clarifies the point, doesn't it?"

7. "So did that address your concerns?"

8. "Did I explain that to your satisfaction?"

9. "Did that clear that up?"

10. "Did I explain that correctly?"

4. Ask For the Sale Again

After overcoming the objection and receiving their confirmation that you have successfully addressed it to their satisfaction, ask for the sale again. If more objections arise, continue to address them using the steps outlined above. You must have their agreement that all their questions and concerns have been addressed or they will not move forward to their purchase.

Quiz time - Some Standard Objections Heard Everyday

This is your opportunity to put into practice what you have learned. After you read each of the following objections or comments, take a moment and practice how you would address them. Write down your reply and then read it aloud. How does it sound to you? How would that sound if you were the prospect hearing it? If you have access to a recording device, use it to record your reply and listen to how it sounds. In the absence of a recording device, try calling your telephone number and leave your response as your message. Think outside the box, as this is incredibly valuable feedback.

The combination of reading, writing and speaking your reply will set it in your memory far more effectively than just thinking about your reply. Several examples of how you can address these standard objections follow at the end of the 20 objections. Practice the 4-step process and use the objection acknowledgement statements you have learned to start your rebuttal. Be TOTALLY HONEST with yourself here. If you can't come up with at least one, if not several, responses to each of these standard industry objections, you are losing sales, and in return you and your company are losing MONEY.

How will you feel if you get one of these standard objections on your next presentation and didn't practice addressing it?

Top 10 Common Sales Objections – Part One

1. "We need to think about it."

2. "I want to shop around."

3. "I have to bring my wife back before I can make a decision."

4. "I like the competitor's model better."

5. "Is that your best price?"

6. "Your price is too high."

7. "That's more than I wanted to spend."

8. "If you take off $2000, I'll buy it."

9. "They have hot tubs at the box store for $5,000."

10. "I want 100 jets in the spa."

Top 10 Common Sales Objections – Part Two

11. "Your competition has a lot more horsepower in their tub."

12. "Full foam is bad, because it's hard to work on them when they leak."

13. "I really want a TV in the spa." (Assuming you don't sell a TV option)

14. "If I can't get it by Friday, forget it."

15. "I don't want to pay until next year."

16. "Do you have a heavy-duty floor?"

17. "Can I stand on your cover?"

18. "Why don't you use the heat from the pumps to heat the tub?"

19. "This spa is too deep for my family."

20. "I need to measure."

Grab a piece of paper and start writing out your responses. Challenge yourself here.

Top 10 Responses to Common Sales Objections

1. "We need to think about it."

***Probably THE biggest objection you will ever get
selling any product, anywhere, at any time.***

The reality is that this is not a specific objection; it is just a stall
tactic to put you off. A true objection is more tangible and specific
than your prospect simply saying, "We need to think about it."
They are hiding the real reason they don't wish to move forward;
you need to find the true objection. If you have built great rapport,
you should get an objection that is far more specific than, "We
need to think about it."

So just where does the objection, "We need to think about it" come
from? Your prospects' individual reasons can be many; it is up
to you to find out. Often this objection stems from the following
areas, which you may be completely unaware of:

- **No Perceived Value in Spa Ownership**

    Rarely is this the case. You have a "destination store,"
    which simply means your prospect seeks *you* out when
    they are interested in your product. You are usually not just
    another store in a major shopping mall that people happen
    to walk in while shopping. The prospect does not recognize
    or place high enough priority on a need to take action. This
    prospect is moved closer to the buying decision through
    powerful benefits. They really need to first be sold on the
    merits of owning a spa, and then sold a spa. You need to
    have a great discovery and YOU need to suggest uses and
    reasons they never thought of in owning a spa.

- ### No Trust in You or Your Products

This one is huge to your prospect and many sales are lost because of it. Focus on this section if you want to increase your sales. Let me paint an exaggerated example so you easily understand the idea.

Imagine you are a very affluent prospect considering purchasing a $200,000+ sports car. You show up to the dealership wearing designer clothes, a very pricey watch, a 3-carat pinky ring and a pair of shoes that cost more than an average persons' house payment. How would you feel when the salesperson walks up wearing wrinkled jeans, a rumpled work shirt, a 3-day old beard and bed-head? What is your first impression?

You tell him what you are considering purchasing a new car and he presents you with your dream car. The pricey Italian hand-rubbed paint job is sprayed with mud, the dashboard dusty and the windows hazy, the seats stained with who-knows-what and the ashtray overflowing with cigarette butts. Underneath all that crap is an amazing machine - the only problem is, it sure doesn't look it. As a prospect looking at this car, how much trust do you have in the salesperson, their products and their store?

Think of yourself, your products and your store as that fine automobile. Is your store perfect in cleanliness and presentation? Are your floors vacuumed, windows clean and sparkling? Is ALL debris on the floors and sales counter cleaned up? Are the bathrooms cleaned EVERY day? Were your display spas immaculate, spotless and free of yesterday's Styrofoam cups and coffee rings? Is your signage fresh crisp and clean or old and tired-looking? Are your signs 10 years old and faded? Is your running tub water clean and clear and smelling chemical free? Did you put your best foot forward in *your* physical presentation? Did you look and act as a professional? No jeans or wrinkled shirts, I hope. It is not uncommon that your prospect does not feel comfortable with you or your store and consequently prefers not to conduct business with you if you and your store don't look trustworthy and professional. What message does your image send your prospect about the quality of your product, follow-up and customer service?

You will probably never know if it was a lack of trust based on an unprofessional store image that lead to your prospect saying, "I want to think about it." Improve your odds by having professional looking staff and a stunning showroom.

Did you establish trust and credibility at the beginning of your presentation and give justified reasons why they can trust you and should want to do business with you? Often your prospect will be reluctant to share their true reasons for not wanting to conduct business with you. Oftentimes, your prospect will tell you what you want to hear only to keep you at arm's length. Perhaps a competitor, that looks and acts professionally, convinced the prospect your store has ongoing customer complaints or that you are going out of business.

Can you believe this one? I was working with a storeowner in British Columbia some years back. The owner was a lovely young lady about 35 - let's call her Jan. Every time I saw Jan, she was always dressed immaculately and carried herself with class and grace. She explained to me the areas of her presentation she felt she could improve on and one of her biggest challenges was getting people to sit in the dry spa. She said rarely, if ever, would people accept her invitation to get in the spa. I explained some techniques that had worked for me in the past and suggested she should lead by example and get in the spa first; done correctly, the prospect *should* follow her lead. Here is the sad, but humorous part, and absolutely true. I suggested we both get in the tub and continue our discussion within the dry spa. She looked at me with a squinted brow and said, "Marco, you want me to get in the spa? Its dusty and I'm wearing black." I now understood why she didn't get anyone in the spa.

Spend a minute or two - no, spend 30 minutes - looking at your store with the critical eye of your prospects and customers. Does your store look professional, like the kind of store people want to spend thousands of dollars in? Do you look like the sales professional they want to conduct business with?

I have had the opportunity first hand to visit many spa stores, probably hundreds of stores if not more, from Canada to Europe. Learn from my experience. First impressions are EVERYTHING in retail, and life. Here is my Top 10 list for creating a messy showroom. (Or more accurately put: "You wonder why the prospect has to think about it." They don't trust you or your store because when you talk about warranty, quality and fine craftsmanship, you and your store don't show it.)

Top 10 Tips for Creating an Unprofessional Showroom Image

1. Messy bathrooms

2. Sloppy handwritten signs

3. Dirty showrooms

4. Cobwebs and water stains on store windows

5. Unkempt staff wearing clothing that belongs in a goodwill store

6. Coffee cups or coffee rings on spas, from two days ago

7. Cheap "stick-on" letters on your store windows or old faded outdated signs

8. Spelling errors on signs (Nope, not kidding)

9. Sales staff that smell like cigarettes and look like hell, chewing wads of gum

10. Running tub has green water, foam and a chemical smell that brings tears to your eyes when you walk in the store

Now I am confident that YOUR store is not like the ones I have mentioned, but if it is, you have some work to do. You might be saying, "Wait, Marco, we are a little Mom and Pop store and don't have big bucks in the budget for all those improvements." Are these "improvements" or common sense cleaning tips? If you put 20 minutes into cleaning your spa and showroom everyday, instead of checking your personal emails and surfing the internet, would you have a cleaner showroom and a more professional image?

- **No Perceived Urgency in Purchasing the Spa**

  Your prospect may not have a need, or may not acknowledge a new need that you created. They feel no immediate reason to do anything about it. The urgency to own a spa may not be on the top of their list, as they will have other things that may take precedence. These prospects are frustrating, because you may get complete agreement about their desire for hot tub ownership, but the timing is never right. It is up to you to build their urgency. How many times have you heard, "I have been thinking about it…for years?" Refer back to the chapter on creating urgency for more details.

- **Perception of Superiority of a Competitor's Offering**

  They may never tell you this straight out, but it may be in the back of their minds if they have just had a very effective presentation from a competitor. It is up to you and you alone to uncover if they are leaning towards a competitor's product. What did they like? What did they dislike? Why didn't they buy when they saw the competitor's offering? At the very least, you should be able to figure out what competitor they visited and be able to point out their weaknesses.

- **Lack of Funds to Purchase the Offering**

  We have touched on this before. If your prospect is in your store, I genuinely believe they are interested in purchasing a spa, whether it is yours or your competitor's. It will all come down to perceived affordability. It will be up to you to understand their unique financial concerns and work within their budgets to get them the right spa for the right price. Yes, there will be the very odd exception when they truly are just killing time while their car is being serviced at the garage next door. Is this a wasted 'up' or prospect? Never - this is a great opportunity to practice all the new techniques you have learned.

False Perception
"It's Safer To Do Nothing" or
Fear of Making Any Commitment

This perception is your prospects' fear of making any decision for fear that it is the wrong decision. Probe and ask questions to fully understand their fears, buying motives and reinforce that their concerns are respected and understood. Remember, they only lack the knowledge and the confidence to move forward with their investment. Only you can reduce those fears and provide justification in their purchase.

- "Have I answered every question to your satisfaction? Is there anything else we can do for you at this time to help you with your decision?"

- "From what you told me about the hot tub that you wanted, I believe we found the model with the features that would best fit you needs. If you don't mind me asking, is there something about the tub that you are unsure of or something I did not explain?"

Acknowledge each response, re-qualify the prospect and sell.

Eliminate any potential "Buyer's Remorse" before it occurs. Refer to Buyer's Remorse page towards the end of the book for additional information. Often in the back of the prospects' mind are these three concerns:

A. Will I get good service? (Sell your company)

B. Is this the right spa? (30-day trial)

C. Is it the money / price? (Did you offer financing?)

Make sure you find the concern and then resolve it!

A. Will I Get Good Service?

Did you do the following:

- Establish sufficient credibility?
- Explain to the prospect that your store as been in business for over __ years?
- Show the prospect your wall of fame?
- Share with your prospect that XYZ Spa Company has been building spas for over __ years?
- Explain your delivery, start-up and ongoing support and FREE water testing is included in their spa purchase?

B. Is This the Right Spa?

Your discovery will have eased many of these fears, as you will have learned everything they ever wanted or needed in a spa.

"Mr. Prospect, from what you told me about your family's hot tub needs, I believe we found the perfect model with the perfect features that would best fit your needs. Why not try out this spa for 30 days in your backyard and if you are not happy with this model, we will pick it up and get you into the model that will make you happy?"

"What day of the week should we set up for the delivery of your spa to start your 30-day in-home trial?"

C. Is It the Money / Price?

Did you mention your various financing programs? Over half the spa purchases in North America are financed. I have had dealers tell me, "Marco, all our clients pay cash or use their credit card for the full purchase." Let's think about that for a moment. If that is the only payment option your prospect has, you are absolutely correct - all your customers *did* pay with cash or credit card, because they had no other choice!

What happened to the prospects that loved you and your spa, but needed financing? Prospects may not ask if you have financing packages out of pride. Instead, they will tell you, "I need to think about it." Offering financing, and having suitable signage with the very visable details, will result in more sales.

If you were a prospect on a tight budget, would a spa sign with bold letters listing the price of $6,999 be as attractive as the same bold sign with "Own this spa for as little as $82 per month"? Want that same prospect to buy your stereo with the finance package? How about another small sign on the spa - "Supersize it, add a stereo for only $9.99 per month"? The prices you quote will need to reflect your individual financing packages and stereo upgrade options.

Oftentimes, you will have to **handhold** your prospect and help them over the hump of indecision.

1. *"Mr. Prospect, either way you want to go is fine with me. I completely understand if you are not comfortable taking advantage of this great sale pricing. You can spend a lot more time shopping around only to arrive at the same conclusion all our owners did, or we can just go ahead and order your spa now."*

2. *"Mr. Prospect, in most cases there are three reasons that hold people back from making a decision to invest in one of our spas. Sometimes they don't understand just what it is we are offering, the second reason is I may not have built enough credibility in our store and our products and, lastly, people simply can't afford our products, as much as they would like to. Just so I can better understand your concerns, do you fit into any of these categories?"*

3. *"Mr. Prospect, I can totally understand your concern and how you feel. In fact, many of our XXX (number) of owners over the past XX years felt the same sense of indecision. Many of those owners went out and got other prices, too. They did their research and weighed it all out and what they found after spending, oh, eight to twenty hours of additional homework and shopping time, is that our value was highest. They received all the benefits you see offered here (point to your quote sheet) from us, but even at a higher or lower price from others, they weren't able to beat the value we could offer."*

4. *"Mr. Prospect, let me ask you a question. Now that you know everything there is to know about our spas and doing business with our company, including our cancellation policy, if you really feel that owning one of our spas is not a good fit, what is the worst thing that could happen if you went ahead with your investment today?"*

5. *"Mr. Prospect, with only a small deposit we can order your spa now and you can take advantage of the special deal / price offered today and not have to worry that you will have missed out on this great opportunity."*

6. *"Mr. Prospect, I understand how you feel. Nobody likes to be taken advantage of. I understand my customers want the very pricing I can offer and that is exactly what I will do for you. You see, our owners are our best advertising; our name will be on your hot tub for many years to come."*

7. *"Mr. Prospect, I completely understand you need to 'think about it.' Just for my own understanding, just what is it you need to go home and think about?"*

8. *"Mr. Prospect, thank you for sharing that with me. If I can you show you how owning one of our spas is completely 'risk free,' would you be interested?"*

9. *"Mr. Prospect, I appreciate how you feel. Many of our owners felt exactly the same way you do now. What they found was only after spending many more hours shopping around and being beat up by salespeople, that we really do offer the best spa for the best price."*

10. *"Mr. Prospect, if you did move forward with this investment
    today, what is the very worst thing that might happen?"*

2. "I want to shop around."

This is a very standard objection you will hear often. A lot will be
determined by your store's philosophy on closing the prospect on
the same day. I personally lean towards closing on the same day
when the prospects excitement is very high; your store may prefer
to do just the opposite. Remember, in your prospects' minds, the
dream of owning a spa may soon become a reality.

Hopefully, you have already learned how long they have been
shopping around. The prospect will often say yours is the first
store they have been to as a method to stall their purchase. If
they are truly set on shopping around, you can't risk offending this
prospect by trying to "hard-close" him. You should know all your
competitors, what they offer and how your products are different
or superior. Recap all the unique features and services that you
and your store offer. It may come down to something as small as
in-store water testing or a 24-hour telephone helpline.

Have an information sheet completely separate from your regular literature with a list of at least 5 reasons the prospect should
be in your spas. Put it on your office paper and included it with
your information package you gave them. Make it easier on your
prospect to purchase your product. If they have arrived home,
after visiting 6 spa stores and now have a 5" thick pile of paperwork to read through, how overwhelmed will they be? If you have
ever shopped your competition for a full day, you know their brains
are swimming in pudding. As you put their informational package together, show them the single sheet and say "Mr. Prospect,
here are the top reasons why we have hundreds (or thousands)
or happy owners. When you get home tonight, grab a glass of

wine with your wife because your head will be spinning and you will have heard ever reason why everyone else has the very best spas. Sip your wine and all you have to do to remind yourself of all the benefits our spas offer is to read this one page. That sounds fair doesn't it"?

Top 10 Responses to "I want to shop around"

1. "I understand, it's a big decision and you want to make sure you get the best spa for your money - do I have that correct? I'm glad you came here first. Let's review the main items we discussed." List all the features and benefits again, especially those that elicited a favourable response. (Review and confirm their acceptance)

2. "Is there anything else you think you might want in your spa?" Discuss any items and remind them of all the features that they thought were terrific.

3. "When we started our business many years ago, we spent a lot of time determining which brand to represent (don't say sell). You see we actually did your homework for you. We spent a lot of time looking at all the big manufacturers, looking for a manufacturer that offered not only the best designs, reliability and warranty, but also the best value to our customers. That's why we sell XYZ spas. You won't find a finer spa for the investment we are asking you to make."

4. "I know that your time is very precious and you're eager to get a spa in your backyard. As it will take about three or four weeks to get it here, why don't we reserve one for you right now and you can take advantage of our special pricing during our weekend sale (assuming you are having a sale)? I'm certain you won't find a more suitable spa out there." Does your store offer a 30-day guarantee? If so, use this to full advantage.

5. "Let's take a moment to really identify what you are looking for in a spa and I'll show you how all the benefits of owning an XYZ spa meet you exact needs." If you are selling a Canadian brand in Canada, or an American company selling American spas, mention it and the fact you won't promote an inferior offshore spa. Be very careful with this one, as you might also be selling an offshore manufactured sauna or gazebo and the prospect may bring this up.

6. "Do you know which other stores you are planning on visiting? We will make you a very educated consumer before you leave our store today and are confident that you will come back to us when making your decision." This reply will depend greatly on when the prospect is looking at making their purchase, which is one of the first questions in qualifying your buyer.

7. "Please make sure that you sit in every seat in each tub you are considering. A wet test is very important in making your final decision. If you wish to return to our store for a private wet test, we would be very happy to accommodate your time frame."

8. "Mr. Prospect, let me take a minute to review the features that are completely unique to our spas."

9. "Mr. Prospect, three things have to happen before most families invest in a spa. Those are like, use and afford. You *do* like the spa we discussed don't you? And if you won a spa in a contest on the radio, you would probably use it if it were in your backyard? Well, that just leaves affordability. If owning this spa means you will be eating macaroni and cheese for the next two years, don't do this (a great take-away can often close the sale). But if you like the spa, would use the spa and it fits safely in your budget, what other concerns do you have?"

10. "Do you like the spa?"

"It's okay."

"Well, okay won't do, it has to be perfect! Would you share with me how I could make it perfect?"

3. "I have to bring my wife back before I can make a decision."

This single and dreaded shopper is more aptly named, the "one-legger." Don't be put off by this situation. Understand ahead of time the chances of closing this prospect on the same day are not as likely as presenting to the couple together, unless of course, there is no significant other. Would you spend thousands of dollars without your partner's input? Probably not a smart bet, if you are like me. Of course my wife would hear absolutely no arguments from me if she came home with a new 60-inch flat screen TV and said, "Here honey - I bought this for you just because I love you."

You can try, with trial closes, to find out if this is a decision your prospect can make alone. You can certainly give a great presentation and even write up the order with the promise you will tear up the paperwork if their partner says no. This will move your one-legged prospect closer to owning the spa mentally. Once you have them on your side, you can coach them on how to sell it to their partner. You will have gained a huge ally and be closer to the eventual sale.

- *"Mr. Prospect, I understand you want to ensure everyone in the family loves the spa. Does this one look like the best spa for you and your family? Do you think your partner would want any other features? If this is the right spa, then all that will be left to do is review the color selection with your spouse?"*

- *"Mr. Prospect, will this be a surprise for your wife or will she come in later to finalize the choices of colors and accessories?" (You just found out if he will later say "I have to ask my wife")*

- *"Mr. Prospect, why don't we pick out the perfect spa for you and your partner, do up the paperwork to take advantage of today's sale pricing, and then arrange a surprise wet test for you both? How surprised and loved will your partner feel?"*

- *"Mr. Prospect, I fully respect and understand your need to discuss this with your partner. Here is what I can do to help you out. I can hold this sale opportunity for you if you put a deposit down and let me know your decision within 24 HOURS. I am sure your partner is not going to want to miss out on this. I am sure that if they were here in your shoes, they wouldn't want to miss out on this offer either. A fully refundable 10% deposit is all we need and we'll reserve this special pricing for you, does that sound fair to you?"*

Try to "hard close" the one-legger and you may be pushing them further away from saying yes and a lot closer to saying NO. Become their best friend and help them to sell the concept to their partner. Test the prospects' sincerity and interest and ask, "If your wife says yes, would you do this?" Really test your prospects' commitment and ask, "In the event your partner says no, then what?"

4. "I like the competitor's model better."

Here is where you really need to know your competition and their weaknesses. Don't ever speak unkindly of your competition, but sell against their weak spots. Every manufacturer has them. In the event you are not familiar with the competitive product they like, start asking questions.

"Mr. Prospect, that is a well-recognized brand. May I ask what it is about that particular model that you liked specifically?"

Following their comments, you can simply reply, "Those are all attractive features, and if you like those, you are going to love these (show your competitive features)."

"Mr. Prospect, you really seem sold on my competitors spa. Do you mind if I ask why you didn't purchase it?"

5. "Is that your best price?"

When your prospect asks if that is your best price, it doesn't always mean they are objecting to the price. They may be trying to understand if that really is your best price or if this situation calls for bartering, like car purchasing. The key here is understanding the motive.

If you immediately drop your price, and they were just "testing the waters," you just lost money and lost face in the prospects' eyes. Stick to your guns on the price. If you truly feel the only way you will close the sale is by making concessions, see if they are receptive to having other items included, such as steps or a cover lifter. Get a commitment in advance that if you can work to reduce the price, they will commit to the purchase.

I personally always ask on just about every purchase I make, "Is that your best price?" I am fully content paying the asking price, but just don't feel right if I haven't asked. Oftentimes I receive a discount just by asking.

6. "Your price is too high."

We often hear this objection in the form of, "I need to think about it." Spend the time asking questions to understand what "too high"

means to the prospect. It may mean something completely different to what *you* think it means. Focus the prospects' attention on
the price difference, if it is a direct comparison to another manufacturers model. Your price may, indeed, be higher than a compet-
ing product, but the difference may not be substantial. Instead of
avoiding the issue, call attention to the amount of difference. Con-
cede that your price is higher, but point out that while the actual
difference in price may be only, say, 15%, the prospect receives
85% more in terms of benefits, features, capacity, or performance
with your product. Make these benefits very clear; explain how
the purchase is not an expense, but an investment. Explain to
your prospect in as much detail as possible how much they can
generate in savings through lower operating costs or an extensive
warranty. Contrast the huge benefits they will receive through the
small additional amount your product may actually cost.

Top 10 Responses to "Your price is too high" - Part One

"Mr. Prospect...
1. ...just how much 'too high' are we?"
2. ...what are you comparing our price to?"
3. ...so does that mean we are never going ahead?"
4. ...is price your only consideration or will quality and service be a factor?"
5. ...is your decision based solely on price?"
6. ...it sounds like you have seen a similar spa at a better
   price?"
7. ...thanks for your honesty. What does too high mean to you?"
8. ...in knowing we are not the cheapest spa company,
   does that mean there is no chance we can ever do business together?"
9. ...you will always find someone who will charge more
   and you will always find someone who charges less. We

will never be the lowest, but we will always be competitive."
10. ...that's great! We never want to be the cheapest."

Price Comparison Strategies

Suppose you finally learn your price is $2,000 too high, in your prospects mind. Break the price difference down into smaller units over the life of the spa. Illustrate how small the actual price of the product is by showing what it would cost per day, per week, or per year amortized over the life of the product. Even tightwads can afford pennies a day to realize their aspirations! Ask them how long they think they will own the spa. If the spa is going to be with them for 15 years, how much is that difference now when broken down monthly? $2,000 divided by 15 years and then 12 months means the price difference actually is a little more than $11 per month. Broken down further into days, they are looking at about 37 cents per day to own the spa. For less than a cup of coffee, they can own the spa they truly want. Breaking a price difference down into smaller and smaller increments is a very powerful closing technique. Confirm the spa they want, and that it's just the price that they are uncomfortable with.

- Remind the prospect that you get what you pay for. Ask the prospect to recall a purchase based on a low price that he or she has later regretted.

- Compare your product directly to a more expensive product. Show how your lower-priced product offers features found only in much more expensive products. This will make your price seems lower, as well as build perceived value.

- Compare results, not just price. Remind the prospect that what really matters are the benefits a product delivers, not just the price paid for the product.

- Make the terms of payment as easy as possible. Use low down payments, finance plans, etc.

- Call attention to the hidden benefits of dealing with you and your company. Explain to the prospect that the price you quote is a reflection of the total value received, including other benefits like dependable service, water testing, and a 24-hour support line.

- Challenge the prospect to make sure he is comparing exact specifications. Mention features that may be different. Ask him to compare quality and workmanship. Many products look alike and may seem "just as good," but in reality are quite different (as I'm sure you'll point out).

- Discuss the drawbacks of purchasing cheaper goods.

Top 10 Responses to "Your price is too high" - Part Two

1. "I understand how you feel, Mr. Prospect. I had the same feeling when we first started representing XYZ spas. When I started to see the true quality, performance, features, benefits, warranty and efficiency, I knew we had made the right choice for our business and our customers. I know you will agree with me that there isn't a better choice for you and your family. Isn't that the kind of product that you want to own?"

2. "Are you more concerned with price than value?"

3. "Quality, service or price - which are the most important to you?"

4. "Of course our prices are higher. Considering the quality of our products, the difference should be much greater."

5. "You know you get what you pay for."

6. "Our price only appears high. Have you factored in every

aspect, such as operating costs, quality, service, workmanship and warranties? If you consider these factors, I think you'll actually find us less expensive."

7. "You can always buy it for less, but will you be getting the quality you want? I doubt it."

8. "Mr. Prospect, what you are probably thinking is that because of the additional investment in an XYZ spa, it must be a better choice for my family's enjoyment. That's the real question, isn't it?"

9. "I am very surprised that our price is higher. I would like to be certain that we're comparing the same products, features, and service."

10. "I'm sure you are aware that there are 'similar looking' products that can be purchased for less money. But will you be receiving the same benefits and quality?"

Even More Effective Responses to "Your Price Is Too High"

1. "The prices are not the same because the quality and service are not the same."

2. "Have you ever regretted purchases based solely on the lowest price?"

3. "Does this spa cost too much, or is it more than you want to spend? Let me explain our attractive terms."

4. "Mr. Prospect, may I ask a question? If both hot tubs were $100, which one would you choose?" More than likely they will say yours when compared to the cheaper spa. "Why would you choose ours?" Hear them out, as they will give you all the reasons they want to purchase your spa.

   "I really like the depth, the construction…(hear them out)

   Confirm, "Mr. Prospect, those are excellent points and the exact reason our spa is perfect for you and your family."

5. "Mr. Prospect, I know $$$ is a lot of money, but do you agree that there is a cost associated to having the ... (fill in all the features they really liked), as well as a LIFETIME shell leakage warranty and five years on parts and labour?"

6. "Mr. Prospect, I am not sure if I can do this, but if I was able to make the numbers work for you and your family on a spa, would you purchase the spa today?"

"The bitterness of poor quality remains
long after the sweetness of low price is forgotten."
– Benjamin Franklin

If they say yes, get ready to start negotiating. If you know you have some money you can shave off the price, you better have a really good reason why you just dropped the price. "Nose-Bleed" drops (big price drops), without justification, convince the prospect that you were initially trying to charge too much money. Tell them the spa they are thinking about might be a floor model or a factory second; you need to explain why you are reducing the price. Get the commitment from them that a better price will earn their business. Price is just one of the many objections that will arise when you work in sales.

7. "That's more than I wanted to spend."

You need to determine is your price too high for the spa they are considering or is it more than your prospect budgeted to spend today. You need to ask how they established their budget.

● "Mr. Prospect, I understand how you feel, things are expensive these days. Can I ask you a question? Is your budget a guideline or an anchor? When I shop I try to set budget range I want to be in. Is this the most you can spend or a range?" The prospect will usually tell you whether it's the most they can spend or a range they're trying to stay within.

- "Mr. Prospect, why not use our money for the next ___ months and keep your money in the bank making interest? We have some exciting financing options."

- "Mr. Prospect, I understand how you feel. I had the same feeling when we first started representing XYZ spas. When I started to see the true quality, performance, features, warranty and efficiency, I knew we had made the right choice for our business. I know that many of owners would agree with me that there isn't a better choice. Isn't that the kind of spa that you really want for your family?"

- "Mr. Prospect, it sounds like we might have built too much spa for you. Which features would you like me to remove?" (This is called a "take-away" and often your prospect won't want to remove anything. It can result in them increasing their budget for fear of losing the features they want.)

Show a spa within their price range or get them to remove features they previously added to lower the price.

Reduce the price difference to the ridiculous - see #6 for breaking down the price.

8. "If you take off $2000, I'll buy it."

Don't immediately drop your price (or, as we say in sales, don't drop your pants) or offer a discount. First establish value and then begin to discuss price. What do you think your prospects' opinion will be if you immediately drop $2,000? Will they feel you were overcharging them originally? Will they then ask for more price drops and concessions? Why $2,000? Why not $1,000 or even $3,000?

If price is the only objection you need to overcome to complete the sale, then it is just a negotiation, nothing more. You need to understand how they came to that figure. In this case it is $2,000, but you may encounter any price. Is it a budget issue, are they just price shopping or are they just asking to see if there is any room to haggle? Some stores I have worked with, a little over 50%, will negotiate on pricing; how much is entirely up to you. What are your store's pricing policies? Are they comparing your spa to one down the street that is $2,000 less?

Top 10 Responses to "If you take off $2000, I'll buy it"

1. "Mr. Prospect, so if I understand you correctly, if this spa was $2,000 less, you would do this right now for your family?"

2. "Mr. Prospect, do you not think the spa is worth the investment we are asking?"

3. "Mr. Prospect, if you were selling your home and I offered you 75% of your asking price, how would that make you feel?"

4. "Mr. Prospect, it sounds like you might have some budget restrictions."

5. "Mr. Prospect, I understand that you want a discount. However, a discount of that size would certainly mean that some of the options you have selected would have to be eliminated. Would you consider…?"

6. "Mr. Prospect, it sounds like I might have built you too much spa for your budget. Which features do you like the least?"

7. "Mr. Prospect, if you need to spend $2000 less, I can show you other models and options to fit your budget."

8. "Mr. Prospect, many salespeople will show an initial price that is greatly exaggerated and often unrealistic. We don't conduct our business that way. Would you have preferred it if I had done that, and then took the $2,000 off?"

9. "Mr. Prospect, other than the $2,000 difference, is there anything else that would prevent you from purchasing the spa?"

10. "Mr. Prospect, do you mind if I ask how did you arrived at a $2,000 discount?"

9. "They have hot tubs at the box store for $5,000."

Like most things, not all products are created equal. They may look the same, but that is where the comparison ends. Let's think about that box store you mentioned. Did you ever walk into the tools section? Box stores have drills that cost $30 and drills that look almost identical for $300. Why do you think there is such a difference for two drills that look the same? The fact is that other than their looks, they are not even close to being the same quality.

There are a lot of factors you have to consider when you are determining the true cost and value of a spa. The hot tub you are considering at a box store may well be quite cheap, but there are other important factors that need to be considered:

- "What are the monthly costs of running the spa? Box store spas are designed to be low in price, therefore the quality of the components are often reflected in the price."

- "You can't wet-test a box store spa. Did you get in the spa? Was it comfortable? Often box store spas are very shallow, but people don't notice it because the spas are on their sides. Take a moment and get into ours, move around

and try each seat. Most box stores have their spas upright
so you can't even get in to see if you fit."

- "Will they come out and service your hot tub or do you
  have to call a 1-800 number? We have trained professionals to look after all your after-market needs. We also can
  offer you a spa that will fit in your budget, complete with all
  the high quality and warranty you should expect."

- "Do they provide free water testing and assistance with
  any issues that come up over the years?" Continue to go
  through the spa's features and benefits and build the value
  of each.

- "Do you know the average box store has over 17,000 products? We are specialists in the pool and spa industry."

10. "I want 100 jets in the spa."

Probe to understand why.

- "Let's first identify which body points you would like to
  target and make sure you have all the jets available to address those areas."

- "You have to be careful in understanding how some manufacturers count their jets. Here at (your store), we follow
  the industry standard that a jet body is one jet. Some of
  our competitors count every hole in the jet body as a jet.
  See this one - they would consider it nine jets, ridiculous, I
  know." Have a sample jet to show your prospect.

- "More jets do not mean better jets. Some companies use
  many small accu-pressure jets to make it look like you are
  getting a lot of jets. We use a variety of different jets in
  strategic positions to give you maximum massage benefits,
  which can be combined with our foot dome therapy option

and spa energizer option for maximum performance."

- "Keep in mind, the more holes you drill into a spa shell the less structural integrity."

- "How realistic is it that every one of those 100 jets will actually even be effective to your specific needs?"

Top 10 Responses to Common Sales Objections - Part Two

1. "Your competition has a lot more horsepower in their tub."

- *"Mr. Prospect, higher horsepower does not mean increased jet performance or efficiency. Some of the larger pumps our competitors use are far less efficient than our pumps. Technology is rapidly changing today - just look at some of the older cars that had massive engines with huge horsepower, they had horrible efficiency and poor gas mileage. Pumps are just one part of the equation to getting a great massage; plumbing size and design also play an important role. PSI at the jets is one of the most important factors when comparing spa pumps. Our spas are reverse engineered, which means they are designed first, then number and type of jets and correct water flow is calculated, and only then the pumps are sized accordingly."*

- *"Mr. Prospect, a lot of our competitors play the horsepower rating game. The truth is most companies rate their pumps on break horsepower; this is just one way to measure horsepower. There is Break HP, Running HP, and Continuous HP. Get your hands in front of the working jets and YOU decide which feels better. We can show you the flow rates of our pumps if that is important to you."*

- *"Mr. Prospect, the XYZ spa company plumbs their spas specifically to attain maximum flow to the jets while using the least amount of energy to operate your hot tub."*

- *"Mr. Prospect, place your hand in front of the jets and feel the pressure. Any more pressure will not be comfortable."*

2. "Full-foam is bad, because it's hard to work on them when they leak?" (Assuming you sell full-foam spas)

- *"Mr. Prospect, full-foam is still by far the best way to insulate a spa. The best brands in the industry use full-foam. Not only does it insulate the spa more efficiently, it also helps lock in the plumbing so that there will be less chance of leaks occurring from water movement."* Hand the prospect a 2-foot length of 2-inch pipe that is two-thirds filled with water. *"Mr. Prospect, hold this. Now imagine holding it for 15 years. That's the weight load the jets experience if there isn't any foam to support the plumbing. Some competitors simply hang their plumbing with zap straps; as the plumbing swings back and forth for years, the straps can eventually cut into the water lines causing leaks."*

- *"Mr. Prospect, full-foam eliminates the empty dead air space under the shell from acting as an echo chamber, which can amplify the sounds of the pumps. Did you ever build speakers when you were a teenager? Remember how a huge empty box was perfect in creating a huge bass sound?"*

- *"Mr. Prospect, our spas are also designed that all cabinet sides have removable panels in the unlikely event a leak does ever occur. You warranty will cover you for a full five years. In the event a repair has to be completed, a qualified technician will conduct the work."*

- *"Mr. Prospect, if dead air space was the best manufacturing method, we would do it, as it's a lot cheaper to build."*

- *"Mr. Prospect, if you really would rather have a spa without the insulation, we can leave it out for you and probably save you several hundred dollars."*

3. "I really want a TV in the spa." (Assuming you don't sell a TV option)

- *"Mr. Prospect, although a TV may sound as a great idea initially, we have deliberately chosen to stay away from them for a couple of reasons. Who will repair the TV when it breaks down? The high humidity and outdoor environment aren't good for video screens. I have heard the failure rate in the industry has been very high."*

- *"Mr. Prospect, did you check the separate warranty for the TV and any audio equipment? Warranties for these items are usually very short, in some cases only six to 12 months."*

- *"Mr. Prospect, we feel that your hot tub should be enjoyed with family and friends as trouble-free and relaxing as possible for many years to come. How relaxed and happy will you feel if one year from now you're sitting there staring at a burnt-out screen? That option is probably worth several thousand dollars."*

- *"Mr. Prospect, you probably already own several nice TVs in your house. Do really need another one?"*

- *"Mr. Prospect, I had a owner that had a great suggestion; he simply rolls his nice 42-inch flat screen TV up to his patio doors, runs the TV through the spa stereo and still gets to enjoy his TV while sitting in his spa."*

4. "If I can't get it by Friday, forget it."

Surprisingly, this is an objection I heard more often than I would have expected, especially around Christmas or New Year's, or just before a big football game. The prospect has been thinking about investing in a spa for several years and now that they have taken ownership in their mind, they want their spa immediately if not sooner.

- *"Mr. Prospect, so if I understand you correctly, if we can get you your spa in time for your hot tub party, you would like to move forward with this?" Do you see how the objection was rephrased to take the time element out of it? The objection was then isolated and then used as a close.*

- *"Mr. Prospect, I understand how you feel. When I finally find the right item at the right price, I always want it immediately, as well. Let me check our inventory list and see what is immediately available." You should know in advance what is on your inventory list and have lead the prospect to what you already have in stock.*

- *"Mr. Prospect, I can call the factory and see what they have in stock. Would a different color be acceptable if they do have one in stock? If they don't have the one you want, I will get a rush order put in, but worst case scenario, isn't it really worth waiting a few weeks to get exactly the spa you want with all the features you are looking for? You'll be enjoying your hot tub for years and you don't want to regret not waiting a couple of extra weeks for the perfect one, do you? You also need a bit of time to make sure your electrical is in and your backyard is ready, won't you?"*

5. "I don't want to pay until next year."

Confirm with your prospect that this is the only concern they have that is stopping them and, if satisfied, they would move forward with the purchase. Do you offer a variety of financing options for your prospects? Over 50% (if I am not mistaken, the number is closer to 70%) of spa purchases are made with financing. If you think all your customers prefer to pay cash, or you don't think you need a finance program, you are losing sales. If you have a finance program, spend some time with the provider of your financing programs to fully understand this valuable tool. There are many creative ways to use financing options as a powerful closing tool.

- *"Mr. Prospect, so if I understand you correctly, if we can show you a program that doesn't require any payments until next year, you would like to move forward with this?"*

- *"Mr. Prospect, let's look at the financing options we can offer. We do offer six months free financing, plus an assortment of other attractive finance plans."*

- *"Mr. Prospect, are you aware that many businesses bury the financing costs into the price of the spa? What seems like a great deal with 'don't pay until next year' may be more expensive than you might realize. If you own your home, you can most likely get a small line of credit at far more acceptable terms than through traditional finance packages."*

- *"Mr. Prospect, if I can arrange a 'No Payment' program for 12 months, would that work for you and your family?"*

Some of these solutions may not work for you, as they will all depend on what unique financing programs you offer, if any.

6. "Do you have a heavy-duty floor?"

What competitor have they been to and what are their weaknesses? See the question as more than just a question about spa bases - it can reveal what competitors they talked with. When you know this, bring up points of weakness in their spas not related to the base.

- *"Mr. Prospect, yes, we have a solid ABS plastic floor as an option for your spa. We also have a less expensive HDPE black base floor."*

- *"Mr. Prospect, we fully seal the bottom of our spas with 2-lb. closed cell foam, which aids in preventing water from absorbing from the bottom."*

- *"Mr. Prospect, due to our unique floor design, we do not feel there is a need for this type of floor."*

- *"Mr. Prospect, some manufacturers don't have small holes drilled into the floor. In the unlikely event of a leak, it is better to have the water drain away from the spa than to have it pool under the spa."*

7. "Can I stand on your cover?"

I loved this question. I would always ask my prospects, "Do you want to stand on the cover?" If you are getting this as a concern, you should know exactly which of your competitors they have visited.

- *"Mr. Prospect, a spa cover is meant to offer great insulation and ease of operation. It's not meant to be walked on."*

- *"Mr. Prospect, all covers absorb some water over the years and an overly thick and heavy cover will not be easy to maneuver and difficult to open. Reinforcing a spa cover so you can walk on it will only add extra weight."*

- *"Mr. Prospect, we offer a premium 4" x 2" taper, which will*

*give you maximum insulation value while allowing rain wa-
ter to easily run off. You can combine this with your choice
of easy-to-use cover lifter systems."*

8. "Why don't you use the heat from the pumps to heat the tub?"

- *"Mr. Prospect, in fact we do. The air controls, which fa-
cilitate air into the jets, draw the warm air from inside the
equipment area. The warm air generated from the pumps
is drawn back into the spa through the jets. XYZ spas have
engineered its spas to operate at maximum energy efficiency. We have hired an independent testing company
to rate our spas on energy consumption. Let me show you
the results." It goes without saying if this is not the case
with your spa brand, don't say or it will bite you later.*

- *"Mr. Prospect, the pumps are designed to move water, not
to be used as heaters; in fact we vent the motors to ensure
they last for years. You have a cooling system on your car
and on your computer. Doesn't it make more sense to keep
the pumps cooler, resulting in a longer life?*

9. "This spa is too deep for my family."

- *"Mr. Prospect, you want to ensure you can sit comfortably
with water up to your neck and shoulders when it's cold
out. You don't want to have to scrunch down in the tub to
avoid the cold wind do you? Did you notice there is also
a cool down seat the kids can comfortably seat on if they
are a little short? Over the next few years, they will certainly grow into the seats and be far more comfortable. Did
I mention the water cushions? It is difficult to realize the*

actual depth of the spa without sitting in it (get them in the tub and show them the water level)."

Also point out the various seating heights and what they will mean to them (all ages can use the spa).

10. "I need to measure."

- *"Mr. Prospect, I understand having the perfect spa fitting into your backyard design is important to you. We don't want to show up at your house on delivery day and realize we messed up the measurements. Why don't we complete the paperwork on your spa so you can take advantage of this special promotion and I will schedule one of the delivery team to visit your house to complete a site inspection? They can help you with all your measurements and confirm that your spa delivery and set-up will be problem free. Remember, all deposits are fully refundable in the event the spa doesn't fit." (If that is your store policy)*

- *"Mr. Prospect, most of our owners are pleasantly surprised to see how little space their new spa actually takes up in their backyard. They are pleased to find out that their spa takes up about the same room as a 36-inch patio table and chairs. Do you have free space the size of a patio table set?"*

Summarizing Overcoming Objections

Remember the four steps:

1. Acknowledge the objection
2. Isolate, indentify and rephrase the objection
3. Overcome the objection
4. Ask for the sale again

Do you now feel more confident that you can address AND over-come objections much easier? Are you more excited to enter into a presentation knowing you are not going to stumble and fumble trying to overcome an objection? Do you understand how master-ing this crucial skill can help close more sales and make you more money? Do you want to earn more money? When is a good time to start earning more money?

Understanding how to overcome objections is absolutely crucial if you are to be the sales professional I believe you can be. This is without a doubt the area where you will see the greatest improve-ment in your sales presentation resulting in more sales. Don't fall back into old habits of trying to ignore an objection; meet it head-on with the confidence and knowledge you will have gained in this chapter. I promise you it will feel very strange at first, as you increase your knowledge and have the courage to try new meth-ods to overcome objections. Always maintain a positive attitude and don't take objections personally.

Take a moment now and write down what you feel you have learned from this chapter and what you will do differently in your future presentations. Make a commitment to yourself to continu-ally improve your presentation. Address objections with a view that they are only questions that if addressed correctly, will result in more sales.

_____

_____

_____

_____

_____

_____

_____

_____

Practice, practice, and then practice some more overcoming common objections. Your replies should easily roll off your tongue. Turn the radio off and practice in the car on your drive to work, practice in the shower - most importantly, just practice! Towards the end of the book you will see a chapter with more Sample Closes. Review, tweak and adjust them to your presentation style.

Notes

_____

_____

_____

_____

_____

_____

_____

_____

_____

_____

_____

_____

_____

_____

_____

_____

_____

_____

_____

_____

Follow-Up

Effective follow-up means bigger paychecks!

Do you take the time after every missed sale and try to analyze what you felt went well and what didn't? There are only two possible outcomes following your presentation: your prospect purchased your products or they didn't purchase your products. Below are two very different follow-ups that address each of these situations.

Just Like Mom Said...
Don't Forget to Say Thank You

Being the eternal optimist that I am, I am confident your prospect has now made their purchase, so you need to follow these essential tips to ensure your owners are:

- Happy and satisfied

- Unlikely to experience "buyer's remorse"

- Happy to provide you with testimonials and future referrals

Let's start with the absolute basics. Did you shake their hands (shake hands with everyone in the family that is there) and actually say, "Thank you for your business, I appreciate it"? No? Why not? I am genuinely shocked how rarely salespeople thank their customers for their business. You earn hundreds of dollars in commissions, if not more with every sale, yet you don't take the time to say thank you? Do you have a store referral plan that you can give them? Do you discuss referrals with them?

Don't let them leave your store without something in their hands other than their paperwork. I always loved to give away the little yellow floating ducks. Your customer will be much more comfortable justifying their purchase if they're holding something more than just a contract that cost them close to $10,000. Giving them something more than just the paperwork to take home will cost you very little, but will be big on the customer service side of things. They're much more likely to focus on the small token item you gave them on their drive home instead of the expensive purchase agreement in the manila envelope.

Be Creative!

Send everyone a thank you card for their business after they leave the store. (Please see my notes in the next section regarding tips on effectively writing these.) Here are a few suggestions for additional ways to say thank you to a customer who just purchased one of your spas:

- Call them the week before the scheduled spa delivery and tell them you have a small gift at the store for them to pick up (this is a chance to up-sell them on additional store products now they are back in your territory).

- Arrange to give them a bottle of wine or sparkling apple juice and a set of plastic wine glasses for their first spa party.

- Call the day before the delivery as you can bet they are VERY excited. Tell them you are equally excited and look forward to hearing about their first spa party. They probably have it all planned out.

- Ask for photographs of their family enjoying the spa and you will not only have a new best friend, you will continue building your collection of happy owner photos for your credibility wall. There is absolutely no better time to ask for photographs or referral letters than in that very first week.

- Show you are even more professional than what they expect. Explain that you will call three days after delivery and see how everything went to do a follow-up and a " Post Delivery" survey.

  - "Was the delivery done in a professional manner?"

  - "Is everything working to your satisfaction?"

  - "Is there anything you do not understand?"

  - "Don't forget to bring in a water sample."

  - "Please contact me directly in the unlikely event you have any concerns."

Problems or issues with any product can and do exist - that is just a fact of life. How well you deal with them is the true test of a professional. By following up, you have the opportunity to fix any issues before they turn ugly and become Buyer's Remorse. Send them a card on their six-month and one-year anniversary and every year after that. The average family moves and purchases a new house every five years. Wouldn't it be nice if all your owners came back every five years and purchased another high-end product without ever going to the competition? On the one year anniversary of their purchase, why not send a Happy Birthday card to your spa? Your owners will not remember the day they bought their spa but they will certainly remember you and the exceptional service you provided.

In the Event They Didn't Purchase...Yet:

In the event they didn't purchase, you still have a very good prospect that needs to be worked. Don't lose track of this prospect as you have both invested valuable time and built a rapport together.

Less than 70% of spa salespeople, or any salespeople, ever follow-up after a sales presentation they didn't close. They believe the "be-back" bus is just around the corner and heading to their neighborhood soon. Well, it probably isn't. I won't say "be-backs" don't exist, they do, but I would rather have five sales and five noes than five sales and five maybes for my own peace of mind. As salespeople, we often count "be-backs" as if it will be a sale. When your boss asks how things are, telling them about all the sales that might "be-back" is unrealistic. A "be-back" is far more likely a lost sale than a sale. I am confident some of you reading this will argue this point, absolutely confident the "be-back" bus is heading your way.

I am reminded of the story of a young man fishing. A stranger approaches and asks how the fishing is. "Great," the boy replies. "If I catch one more fish and then three after that, I'll have four." It is not a sale until it is a sale.

You just spent one to two hours getting to "I'll think about it" and now putting in that extra 15 minutes of great follow-up seems like too much hard work? Fear of rejection will hold you back from making more money and is usually the underlying reason behind a lack of follow-up. The selling doesn't stop when the prospect says "NO" or "I want to think about it" and leaves your store, unless you believe it is over.

You will significantly increase your spa sales and customer satisfaction when you follow-up professionally with everyone, whether they buy from you or not.

What do you have to lose?

Remember, people buy you first, and then your product. Your prospect can't help but be impressed when you follow through and do what you promised, which is follow-up. Great follow-up is a reflection of your professionalism and of the store you work for.

If you want to make more sales resulting in more money, you need to follow these simple steps. You need to set yourself apart from your competition and great follow-up is one of the ways to do this. If your prospect ends up buying a competitor's product and is dissatisfied, you might just be the salesperson they will eventually recommend to their friends when they are considering a spa purchase.

Step One - Obtain Your Prospect's Contact Information

Obtaining your prospect's contact information is crucial to running a successful follow-up program. No contact information, no follow-up. The following ideas will assist you greatly when asking your prospects for their contact information.

Option A

"Mr. Prospect, occasionally we have a blemished spa or a last minute promotion from the factory that could result in great savings to you. Would you like me to let you know if one of those comes along?"

This will really give you an idea if your prospect was truly serious or just tire kicking. After all, anyone looking to spend big money on a high-ticket item would love to save some money - wouldn't you?

Ask them if they wouldn't mind giving you their telephone number so that you can call and follow-up with them. Many of those who aren't qualified buyers won't give you their contact information.

Option B

Another approach to see if your prospect is serious is to ask if you can follow-up to answer any questions that usually pop up after they leave the showroom.

> *"Mr. Smith, when can I follow-up with you to answer any questions you might have? I can call you on Tuesday afternoon or Wednesday evening, which one is best for you?"*

This phrase is very powerful. Wait for your prospect to respond with a time and method for you to contact them. Create a list of names to follow-up with. You will not only appear very professional, you will set yourself apart from other spa salespeople they have talked with.

Ask the prospect what is the easiest way to reach them. They will usually give you a telephone number or perhaps an email address. After they are comfortable giving you their telephone number, ask their mailing address. Should they be uncomfortable, simply explain that you wanted to send them a thank you card.

Option C

Leave them a quote sheet outlining the spa and features you have discussed and ask them to complete the top portion with their contact information. You get a copy and they get a copy. Point out this information will be kept on file in the event they should return to the store and you are not available; the store staff will have all the information at hand.

Step Two - Send a Thank You Card Within 24 Hours

A thank you card is one of the most impressive parts of great follow-up because you did what you promised. It must NOT be forgotten.

Prospects will rarely expect you to actually take the time to send them a thank you card. When it shows up in the mail, they will be reminded that you and your company go above and beyond the norm to truly take care of their prospects. Remember, if they have been to three, four or even five spa stores, their heads are spinning with information and everyone's spa looks the same. How well do you think you stand out from your competitors if you have given a great presentation, built warm rapport and sent them a thank you note when none of your competition did?

Some tips for writing a great thank you card are:

- Handwrite the note to give a personal touch.

- Refer to a personal comment said during your presentation, eg., 'Shirley, you mentioned the arthritis pain in your neck."

- Use proper grammar and spelling – it is important!

- Don't include any professional letters or business cards.

Sample:

"Hi, Mr. Smith, it was a pleasure to meet you and your wife Kathy.

I look forward to helping your family find just the right spa for your backyard vacation! I know a spa will really help give you relief from your lower back pain."

Cheers,

Marco Longley

Step Three -
Calling Your Prospect

This is probably one of the biggest anxiety-inducing events that sales professionals face. What do you say if they pick up the phone? What do you say if they don't pick up the phone? Calling to follow-up with your prospect is absolutely necessary, especially if you have given your word that you will call. Call your prospect on the specified day (make sure you call them within a week if no specific day was set). Again, like the thank you card, this shows your professionalism and attention to detail and your follow through.

Write down in advance what you are going to say and practice your telephone pitch before you actually make the call. Keep some notes to refer to, in addition to your planned comments, to help make the call easier. Call your cell phone and practice leaving your message, so only you will have the opportunity to play it back and hear how you actually sounded. You will be amazed at how different and confident your voice and message sound, after leaving yourself a message only five or six times. Don't forget to make this call.

I am often asked when the best time is to make follow-up calls to a prospect you didn't close.

The answer is quite simple: *two minutes after you have just sold another spa.* What mood are you in immediately after selling a spa? You just sold a fully loaded spa, completed the paperwork and sent the happy customer out the door with yellow ducks and a contract. If you are like me, at *that* moment you are bulletproof and you can walk on water. You are "hot stuff" and already mentally spending the big commission cheque you just earned. All that energy and enthusiasm will transfer through the phone and directly to your prospect you haven't yet sold. Call them! Sell them!

Try the following telephone dialogue:

> *"Hello Mr. Smith, its Marco with (your store name). We met last Tuesday when you were in our showroom and you asked me to call you today and follow-up. I'm ready for your questions."*

Or

> *"Hello, Mr. Smith, its Marco with (your store name). I am calling you as I promised I would. When you were last in the store, we discussed setting up a wet-test for later this week. Would Wednesday or Friday be better for you and your family?"*

Or

> *"Hi, Mr. Smith, this is Marco with (your store name). You asked me to call you if a great deal came up on one of our spas. Well, it's your lucky day and I have some very exciting news. I just learned our factory is having a big promotion on the circulation pump and the ozonator you liked so much. The promotion is for this weekend."* (Choose any suitable option. You don't even have to be having a promotion on that option, but you better include it at a special promotional price when your prospect comes back in or risk losing all credibility.)

Or

> *"Hi, Mr. Smith, this is Marco with (your store name). We have a scratch-and-dent spa we are going to blowout this weekend, so I thought I would offer it to you first before the weekend."*

Step Four –
Follow-Up Telephone Calls, Letters or Postcards

Bruce P. in Winnipeg, Canada, sells 100+ spas every year, working part-time. He is one of the very best spa sales professionals I ever worked with. He takes control from the minute a prospect walks in the door. He sits them at his desk and the very first thing he does is get all their contact information. I mean everything, right down to their cellphone numbers. Only after he has all their contact information does he start his presentation.

I almost fell over when I saw Bruce do this, as it is completely opposite to the presentation I am comfortable using. The interesting thing is, Bruce's method works for Bruce, but it wouldn't work for me, as it doesn't match my selling style. It may or may not suit your style either, you'll only know if you give it a try.

The most impressive part of Bruce's professionalism is his collection of prospect folders. At any given time, he has at least three 3-inch binders of literally every prospect he has talked to in the past three years. I worked a tradeshow with him and saw firsthand prospects approaching our display booth and heard time and time again about how often Bruce kept in touch, even if they still weren't ready to purchase. I also had the opportunity to meet several of his existing owners at the show, and they were equally effusive of his continued contact. One of the keys to his success is that he always asks permission first, to call and to keep in touch with them.

He only removes their names from his "prospect list" under a couple of special circumstances.

1. If they said they were no longer interested in purchasing a spa

2. If they purchased a competitor's spa (but only after a fact-finding telephone call to understand what type of spa they bought and why they preferred it to his spas). Of course, hearing they purchased a competitor's spa, he would congratulate them on their purchase of a spa, thank them for considering an XYZ spa and remind them that they are still welcome to bring in water samples for free testing and grab a coffee. Often this would lead to chemical sales for his store, in place of the spa sale.

Something very interesting happens to prospects that purchase a spa from a competitor. Often, they are embarrassed to go back into the store they didn't purchase from (yours) and ask for free water testing. Even if they live a block away from your shop, they may avoid your store and drive elsewhere for water testing. However, if you have been polite and professional and have invited them back to your store, you have a far greater chance to earn their business selling them other products, such as chemicals. If the spa they purchased works perfectly for them, you still get a shot at the spa chemical sales. If the spa turns out to be a lemon, you are still seen as the hero who tried to help and may win back any referral business.

Bruce learned from polite probing questions what his prospects saw in a competitive product and adjusted his presentation to reflect his newfound knowledge. He would also remove their names after they purchased one of his spas and transfer them to his follow-up file for owners. Can you imagine what it would feel like to sell 100 spas working part-time? Learn from Bruce's examples, I know I have.

Wish you were Here

Want to be creative? Send a specialty postcard with a picture of your hot tubs (you can make your own postcards on the computer) to your prospect, write on the back, "Wish you were here," along with your name and a personal comment.

Build Your Lead Follow-Up System

Building your own follow-up system may be time consuming, but will be well worth the effort as it keeps you on track and up-to-date. Keeping a "check-off list" to attach to each prospect's contact information reminds you of where you are in the follow-up process. You should also have jotted down a few personal notes about the prospect shortly after they left. It might be their children's names, a job title or anything else you remember to make it personal. You can use a clipboard, notes in your 3 ring binder or a follow-up card as shown below.

Action	Timeframe	Comments
Thank You Card		
Follow-Up Call		
Letter		
Other		

Turn an Active Prospect Into an Owner

Only by keeping a follow-up list of active prospects, can you turn those prospects into owners. Keep in touch and don't stop contacting them until they tell you to.

Follow-Up Every Sale with a Follow-Up Offer!

Many salespeople are so happy for one sale; they cringe at the thought of following up with the same owner with yet another offer. I admit there is a special finesse to doing this correctly, as it is not for the faint of heart. Offer them something that is related to their original purchase that they really liked, but didn't purchase. After a few days, when they have completely taken ownership in their minds, call back and sell them the item they really loved, perhaps a stereo.

How about something like this:

> "Mr. Smith, something very interesting just came to my attention today and I wouldn't feel right if I didn't share it with you. I just learned that next weekend the factory will be having a special promotion on our spa stereos and they will be at a discounted price. I know you were very interested in a stereo on your new 'Alpha Moonbeam,' spa but the numbers just didn't work out for you and I completely respect that. If you are still interested in adding a stereo for the upcoming promotional price, we still have time to adjust your order and add a stereo for only $XXX."

If you can do this successfully, congratulations; there probably is not much more I can share with you regarding sales.

After putting into action what you've discovered in this chapter, you will see that a great follow-up will result in more sales, more referrals AND happier owners!

To Recap

- Send a thank you card within 24 hours of their visit.

- Call within seven days to get them back in the store to see you, or at their home to do a site inspection / recommendation.

- Send a letter within 30 days of last contact if you have not heard from them.

- When you do make the sale, send them a thank you card for their business. Follow-up calls should be made before and after delivery and notes sent at six and 12 months post sale.

Notes

_____

_____

_____

_____

_____

_____

_____

_____

_____

_____

_____

_____

_____

_____

_____

_____

Extras

Transition Statements Recap

Transition From Your Greeting Into Your Credibility - Page 55

"What have you heard about our store?" (Use your store name for added branding)

"Mr. Prospect. Before we go look at our spas, if you are like most people, you probably have two questions. What spa am I going to buy, and from whom am I going to buy it from? Does that sound about right?"

Transition From Credibility to Discovery - Page 74

"Mr. Prospect, in order to better understand your needs plans and what is important to you, do you mind if I ask you a few questions?"

Transition from Discovery to Presentation - Page 77

Recap your dialogue with your prospect to prove you have listened to what they said and are sincerely interested in addressing their needs. Show them you are the expert and they will follow your lead.

"We" Mr. Prospect, if I understand you correctly, you are looking for _____ and you need it because _____.

You have 3 kids and need seating for _____. You already have addressed the electrical details." (Recall all the details you learned in your discovery that are important to your prospect). "Do I have that correct? I am sure we have just the right spa for you and your family over here. Please follow me as there are a few great ideas I would like to show you that would fit your needs perfectly."

OR

"Well Mr. Prospect, you have really given me some great information (doesn't everyone like to think they are not only being listened to, but actually heard), which will allow me to make some terrific suggestions. Let's begin over here".

Transition from Presentation to the Close - Page 159

"So Mr. Prospect, you now have a better understanding of who we are, what we do and how we do it. If I understand your needs correctly, it looks like the model ABC will suit your family the best (recap why they want a spa). Do I have that correct?

At this point, go into your close using the examples I have provided.

Buyer's Remorse

Buyer's remorse is an emotional condition whereby a person experiences feeling a bitter regret or a feeling of guilt associated with a purchase. Buyer's remorse is an anxiety inducing feeling your prospect has made a horrible mistake. While not limited to, buyer's remorse is usually associated with high-value items.

We have all experienced buyer's remorse at one time or another. Maybe I should have purchased the blue color, or maybe the larger model in green. How about being in a nice restaurant and wishing you had ordered a different meal after you see your friend's big plate of BBQ ribs arrive? Or perhaps one of your friends buys the same item you purchased last week, only they found it for 20% less. We have all experienced that familiar pang of doubt in the pit of our stomachs. Buyer's remorse is easy to overcome with the correct approach.

So you have sold a spa or pool and now you must wrap-up the paperwork in a professional manner and send your customers on their way. After I receive a "Yes, we'll take it," and before I complete the paperwork with a prospect, I try to always ask, "Do you mind if I ask why you did this today for your family?" You will hear all their big hot buttons and motivators, stated by them, usually in three or four sentences (remember to add this to your customer file). Confirm with the prospect those are terrific reasons, their family will have years of enjoyment from their investment today. This will serve to reinforce and justify that their decision was sound. "Speak now, or forever hold your water" was a personal favourite comment at the exact time of their signatures; this simple sentence is far more disarming than most people ever realize. Didn't I just tell them if you sign the paperwork, it's a done deal?

Only after all the paperwork has been completed and the prospects' credit card or cheque book put away, should you mention any potential remorse that might pop up. Don't plant negative seeds, or seeds of doubt; instead, address that they may feel a slight twinge of anxiety at some point. Confirm with them exactly why they did what they did today. Reinforce the benefits they will receive based on their investment with you today.

"Mr. Prospect, you have done a very special thing for your family today. Occasionally, not very often though, I have heard of owners waking up in the middle of the night, thinking about their investment today or that their kids might have massive hot tub parties while they are away. In the unlikely event you wake up at 3:00 a.m., thinking about your hot tub and pool parties, chuckle to yourself and try to go back to sleep."

When to address and put buyer's remorse to rest really will depend on how solid you think the deal is and if it will really stick or kick. In some cases, you will have connected extremely well with your customers. In other cases, the connection, even though they purchased, may feel a bit stiff and awkward; you may wish to touch on buyer's remorse with them. If you feel the deal might kick, don't be afraid of calling your new owner and asking, "Mr. Prospect, it has been a couple days since you were last in the store. I just wanted to follow and see if you had any questions since I last saw you."

Notes

_____

_____

_____

_____

_____

_____

_____

_____

_____

_____

_____

_____

_____

_____

Notes

Effective Price Presentation

There is only one *right time* to talk about the price of your products. That is when you are confident your prospect will see that the value and benefits of ownership exceed the price you ask. When you finally present your price, look into their eyes, say the price as though the product were worth 10 times what you're asking and translate the investment price into value. Your prospect can smell fear a mile away and if you lack confidence or get weak or soft when presenting the price, your prospect will quickly see this and may get spooked. If you appear uncomfortable, they may question if your offer really has good value because you don't seem to have confidence the offer, so why should they.

Deal with price last. Any price, out of the context of what your product does for your prospect (the benefits), is too high in their mind. Don't be lured into a discussion of price before you learn what your prospects' needs are and how your product's benefits will fill those needs. You must first establish value in order to justify your asking price. Recall the example of the MARCO1606 dive helmet; only after the benefits were explained and acknowledged, did the price seem more reasonable. If you bring up price too early, you will spend the rest of your presentation trying to justify your price instead of focusing on the benefits of your product, which will justify the price.

How many times have prospects walked up and asked, "How much is this one?" and you immediately gave them the price? Why? If your prospect doesn't completely understand what benefits your product offers, they will have a very difficult time in accepting the price you just quoted; you are starting off on the wrong foot. You have lost control of the presentation before it has even started by telling them the price. This question gives you a huge opportunity to get into your presentation as the prospect has given you permission to ask questions by first asking you, "How much is this one?"

Top 10 Responses to "How much is this one?"

1. "That is a great question. It sounds like you are genuinely interested in getting a spa for your family. Do I have that right? Are you familiar with our spas? No? Well, let me tell you a bit about ourselves and the spas we carry."

2. "Mr. Prospect, you are on page 27 and I am only on page 18. I'll address your price question in just a moment; before I do, there are a couple of key features I would like to show you first." Take control away from your prospect and return to your presentation where you left off. This is suitable if you are part way into a presentation and the prospect tries to take control of your presentation.

3. "Mr. Prospect, would you agree that if the hot tub doesn't do everything you need it to do, the price really doesn't matter then, does it? Let's take a moment and find out what is important to you and your family."

4. Say very casually, "Depends," and shut up. Your prospect will have no choice other than to either be quite or ask, "Depends on what?" If they ask, then you are once again back in control.

5. "Which options do you want?" If they are pushing you to give up a price, when you ask them what options they want you will usually get a blank stare, as they will have no idea what their choices are.

6. "Mr. Prospect, how many would you like?" (Obviously said

with humour, unless you're really good and can convince them that you offer a "contractor's" discount if they purchase two - one for the main house and one for the cottage.)

7. "Mr. Prospect, that is a great question. I love direct people. Which one would you like me to wrap up for your family?"

8. "We have a two-for-one sale today. In addition to this one, which other one would you like?"

9. "We sold that one yesterday. It was $99." This is said just to test your prospects' reaction and see if they are listening. Again, you can't pull this comment off unless you have a strong and playful rapport with your prospect.

10. "Gee, I am not really sure; I can look it up for you. Is this one you want or would you prefer a show you a few other choices first?"

Notes

_____

_____

_____

_____

_____

_____

_____

_____

_____

_____

_____

_____

Breaking the Prospects' "Pact"

The prospects' pact is an agreement they have made that they simply refuse to move forward with a purchase on the same day they met you. It is a safety net they set up so their partner will not commit to a purchase, even though they may each absolutely love the idea of the investment and would move forward with the purchase if their partner agreed and there was no pact.

"Mr. and Mrs. Prospect, I would like to share with you something very interesting that I have occasionally noticed with our customers. I have had a couple of owners of mine say that they sat in their car before entering our store and made an agreement. It sounded something like this, "Honey, I don't care what the salesperson shows us, it doesn't matter how good the deal sounds or how well it will suit our needs, we are not making a decision today." Does that sound familiar? Well, if it did, that's okay, it's very common. Sometimes my wife and I will do the same. We have learned over the years that making our pact and closing our minds off before we even see what our options are, may not be in our own best interests after all. Mr. Prospect, how does this sound? I'll explain who we are, what we do and why we do it. After that, if what we are offering makes sense to you, is completely affordable and meets all your needs, it's okay to do this for your family today. Does that sound fair to you?" Ask both husband and wife if it is fair and shake their hands in agreement.

As you go through your presentation, get confirmation statements from both partners. Each partner must be treated individually and not as a couple. "Mary, what do you like the most from what we have talked about so far? And John, what do you like the most?"

You goal is to get both of them on the same page and in agreement.

As each hears the other responding favourably, each thinks "Hey, this isn't what we agreed to in the car, but I guess my partner has changed their mind and it is okay to do this today." With each separate agreement, the pact softens and you are far likelier to close the sale.

Notes

_____

_____

_____

_____

_____

_____

_____

_____

_____

_____

Top 10 Power One-Liners

1. "Few sounds are more relaxing than that of running water."

2. "Melt away your muscle strain and stresses."

3. "Indulge yourself with a daily massage in your own backyard."

4. "Enjoy a stress-free vacation just steps from your back door."

5. "Soaking in hot water feels sooo good."

6. "Our spas invigorate and soothe your senses."

7. "It's naked time!"

8. "Don't play leg spaghetti with a small spa."

9. "The jets relax your muscles while the lights soothe your mind."

10. "In Roman times, people came from far and wide to get a glimpse of the spectacular Roman baths - you just have to walk to your backyard."

Top 10 Sample Closes

1. Feel, Felt, Found

This is probably one of the oldest and well-known closes. Used correctly, it is extremely effective at helping overcome your prospects' objection and move them forward with their buying decision by associating with like-minded customers.

The first step upon hearing their objection is to empathize with them. Let them know that you completely understand how they *feel*. Share with them an example of previous owners who *felt* the exact same way they do now and then explain to them what the other owners did to resolve or address the situation or objection, explain what they *found*.

> *"Mr. Prospect, I can totally understand your concern and how you feel. In fact, many of our owners over the past 10 years felt the same 'need to shop around' as you have right now. Many of those owners went out and did their research, received other price quotes and weighed it all out. What they found after spending, oh, eight to 20 hours of additional homework and shopping time, is that we offered the highest value and most benefits. Those owners received all the benefits you see offered here (point to your quote sheet) from us, but even at a higher or lower price from other stores, they weren't able to beat the value we could offer."*

Why does it work?

We all like to be acknowledged when we voice a concern. We want to not only be heard, but fully understood as well. In empathizing with your prospect on how they feel, you are working together to resolve a condition and you are continuing to build rapport. Explaining how other owners felt the same way, helps them "connect" with a group of wise purchasers; they don't feel alone. In explaining how the "group" adjusted their thinking and found the purchase made sense, your prospect will often fall in line with this thinking.

2. The Alternative Choice Close

Another "oldie, but a goodie," the Alternative Choice Close is extremely effective. Rather than asking for the sale, you close the sale at both responses.

> *"Mr. Prospect, would you like the ABC model with or without the lounger?" or "Do you want me to include the free steps or the free cover lifter?"*

Notice the prospect doesn't have the option of saying no. Both statements are assumptive closes and if the prospect doesn't wish to move forward with their purchase, they must stop you.

3. The Puppy Dog Close

If you take the puppy home for the weekend, you own it. You are not likely to return it. Professional salespeople know if the prospect takes a product home for a 30-day trial, 98 per cent of prospects will keep it. If you offer such a 30 day program, get your prospect to purchase on approval. If they feel there is limited risk with their investment, why wouldn't they move forward with their purchase?

4. A Good Story Close

Everyone loves a good story, especially with a happy ending. Prospects learn very well through stories rather than just "telling." Your stories will sink into their subconscious minds. Stories sell! Work with your staff to develop some great stories to deal with common objections (price, value, procrastination or taking action). Recall the story of Dan the carpet layer and his volleyball knees.

5. The Invoice Close

One of the most effective closes is simply to begin completing the invoice. Occasionally ask confirming questions, i.e. "the correct spelling of your name is…." Don't say anything at the end, just hand over the completed form and your pen and show them where to sign.

6. Get Six "Yeses" and You Should Get the Sale

Master sales professionals realize the power of habit and conditioning. If they can condition their prospects to say yes repeatedly, when the close finally comes, they'll be more likely to say yes. Get your prospect warmed up and ready to say yes with small questions. Ask questions you know will be answered with a yes. The more "yeses" you receive relating to the sale, the better your closing chances. These are also called "tie-downs."

Ask, "Don't you like the serene feel of the waterfalls?" or "Is this the color blue you wanted?" With each yes, your prospect is taking mental ownership and reaffirming his or her own need. Remember, no one buys financially until they have bought emotionally.

7. "Because You're Serious" Close

In order to avoid your prospects' stalls, get commitments and have the prospect state exactly what they like and what they don't like.

"Mr. Prospect, would I be correct in asking if you "need time to think about it"; you are serious, aren't you? You wouldn't just be trying to get rid of me, would you? Just so I can make sure you have all the information in order to think about it, you do like the idea of owning a spa don't you? What did you really like most about what we talked about today? And

what do you feel are areas that might be a concern?"

Many prospects believe they can blow you off with, "I want to think about it." This is far too vague and with practice, you can engage them in the thinking process and try to draw out more information from them.

8. The "Columbo" Close
Selling situations make people feel pressured. After you've asked for the sale and received a negative answer, the prospect usually lets his guard down and relaxes. This close relies on that relaxation. As your conversation ends and you are walking your prospect to the door, say, "Just between us, and so I can improve my presentation, what is the real reason you didn't do this?' When you hear the reason, start re-selling and close. The latter part of this close is also called the "Hat-in-Hand" Close.

9. The Minor Question Close
This technique is similar to the Alternative Choice Close. The difference is you ask a processing question, not a choice of two items. Here are some examples of processing questions:

- "Is your name spelled with a 'T'?"

- "Is it okay if we deliver it on Saturday?"

- "Did you want us to coordinate matching the cover to the siding?"

The response to all these questions is a purchase.

10. Handshake Close
Extend your hand for a handshake while making a closing offer. Use a big nod and smile as if they have already said yes. Look expectantly. If necessary, raise your eyebrows slightly.

"So, Mr. Prospect, (extending your hand) does that sound fair to you?" "Well done, you are going to love your new hot tub."

People naturally reach to shake your hand when it is extended. Use this to your advantage and use a handshake to close the sale.

Notes

_____

_____

_____

_____

_____

_____

_____

_____

_____

_____

_____

_____

In Closing

Well, there you have it. Congratulations - you finished the book. Self realization is a great motivator. You invested in this book because you realized you wanted more sales; self motivation is even more important than realization. You will have discovered an incredible amount of information in this book, which when practiced and applied effectively, *will* make you more money. If you will recall, this was my motivation in writing this book and your motivation in owning it.

"Continued learning" is the mantra of any true sales professional; continued learning is paramount to continually challenging and improving your position in life. The faster you put these proven techniques into practice, the sooner you will start making more money. There are no more excuses from now on. You have the knowledge. You need only have the courage to step up and out of your comfort zone and apply new ideas and strategies. Only after reading the material in this book, and practicing the exercises and your presentation over and over again, will the words and concepts become part of you and your presentation.

We all live in a very busy world; continued reading and learning can sometimes result in a time crunch. The very best sales professionals in the world are always learning and building a library of sales tools. Some *read* to obtain new knowledge, some prefer *listening* to audio presentations while in their cars, while others prefer *attending* sales seminars and workshops. If you have found this book helpful in generating more sales, why not build on that foundation and continue to increase your earning power?

Start building a reference library of informational and motivational authors.

This book is also available in an audio format so that you can continue learning the material while sitting in traffic, waiting at an airport or working out at the gym. The more frequently you expose your conscious and unconscious brain to new material, the more it will stick. How many hours of your week are spent sitting in traffic or on an exercise machine at the gym? Turn the radio off and use that time as your own "University of Learning." My birthday wish list to my friends and family is always the same, year after year - any book, CD or seminar on sales and marketing. Even after being in sales since the tender age of 14, I continue learning and I am always looking for new ideas and strategies to improve my sales performance.

If after reading and applying these techniques, you sold just one more spa, pool or luxury item, the investment you made in this book, and in yourself, would have paid your investment back many times over. If you increased your yearly sales by 20% (many of my students tell me this is easily accomplished), I am confident the difference in your income would be substantial. ***The results you receive will be in direct proportion to your investment in yourself and career.***

Now, I wouldn't be a very good sales professional if I didn't ask you for your continued business. My website offers many exciting and effective sales tools to help you continue your mastery of sales and increase your earning potential. If you haven't attended one of my full-day sales seminars, consider investing in my home study course, assuming that making more money is important to you.

Thank you for allowing me to be a part of your ongoing success. Don't forget to share your personal stories and experiences, so that I might share with others.

Lastly, did you figure out the 'Three Simple Words' that will immediately increase your sales? Simply add 'for your family' when
asking for the business. If the prospect says no, they are saying
no to their families and not you.

Happy Selling!

Enjoy. Learn. Share. Prosper.

Marco Longley

Your Thoughts

_____
_____
_____
_____
_____
_____
_____
_____
_____
_____
_____
_____
_____
_____
_____
_____
_____

Glossary

Active listening
An increased level of your listening capacity. You are actively listening to better understand how your prospect feels about what you are presenting.

Added value
The additional benefits your prospect will gain in conducting business with you and your store. Your prospect will often pay more for your product whether the benefits are real or perceived. Your 24 hour support line or free water testing can be considered added value.

Advantage
This is the 'what does it do' component of the FAB statement. Highlight your unique features through their advantages over your competition.

Benefit
This is the 'what's in it for me' component of the FAB statement. How will your prospect benefit in owning your product? Prospects will buy products or services based on the benefits they will receive through ownership.

Be-backs
Prospects that promise they will be back to purchase. This is a method prospects use to keep you at arms length and rarely do be-backs occur.

Buying signal
A buying signal is a positive verbal or non-verbal indication of your

prospects interest in purchasing your product or service.

Buying temperature
This is an indication of your prospects readiness to purchase. It is usually indicated as hot, warm or worse case, cold.

Close/closing
The close is the final, although not always last step, in the selling process. This is the not to be confused with the 'trial close'. The close of the sale asks the prospect for a buying decision.

Closed questions
Questions that usually results in a 'yes' or 'no' answer. Often used to confirm or 'tie down' your prospect. The opposite of the closed question is the open question, which is asking to elicit more information or details from the prospect. These questions often begin with when, who, where, what.

Closing questions
Closing questions asks for a final decision from the prospect. Not to be confused with trial closing questions, which ask for your prospects opinions or feelings. See Trial closes.

Collaborative selling
Collaborative selling consists of a collaborative effort between seller and buyer.

Concession
An element of the sale with value, either real or perceived, that the seller (more often than the buyer) is prepared to give away. A concession is usually offered with an expectation of receiving something in return.

Consultative selling
Similar to collaboration selling, based on involvement with the buyer through a series of specific questions asked to gain additional useful information.

Customer
The term for your prospect after they have purchased products or services from you or your company, previous to their purchase they are a prospect, or potential customer.

Deal
A standard business term meaning the sale, transaction or purchase.

Demonstration
The physical demonstration of your product or services to your prospect. The product presentation should include FAB statements explaining how a product works and the benefits received. Focusing on your products USP should be addressed in this section.

Enthusiasm
A lively interest, eagerness or zeal

Empathy
Understanding the feelings and attitudes of another person and reflecting these back to the other person. Being able to show and feel empathy is a central focus in more modern selling.

FAB statements
Presentation of the features, advantages and benefits of your product. The statements linking the products physical features to their function and to their eventual benefit. Common and effective technique used in product presentations.

Feature
A physical component of your product that is usually tangible in nature. This is the "What is it" of your products components.

Intangible
An aspect of your product or service that has value, but not in a tangible form, capable of being touched or seen.

Introduction or greeting
The initial phase of a face-to-face meeting

Lay down
Sales that occur in spite of your best efforts to screw them up.
Actually they are sales that occur with minimal effort on your part
and minimal resistance of your prospects part.

Listening
A key skill in successful selling. In the absence of listening skills,
the questioning or discovery phase of a presentation is useless.

Negotiation
The exchange of concessions by both parties to reach an agreement that is acceptable to both the seller and the buyer.

Objection
An objection is the resistance presented by your prospect to stop
the sale from moving to completion. While price is usually the
most common reason for an objection, objections can occur at
anytime for any reason.

Opening
The first stage of the actual sales presentation following the greeting.

Open question
Questions asked to elicit more information than just a yes or no
answer from the prospect. Open questions often begin with when,
who, where, what.

Overcoming objections
Firstly, the technique of mutually understanding the reason for the
prospects objection and secondly using a strong rapport coupled
with fact finding questions to address the objection to the prospects acknowledged satisfaction.

Passion
Powerful or compelling emotions or feelings

Perceived
How something the salesperson said or presented is seen or believed by the prospect. The prospects belief of what the item or comment really means to them.

Preparation
The work, study and preparation that is completed in advance of a meeting with a prospect for the purpose of engaging them in the purchase of your products.

Presentation
The physical demonstration of your product or services to your prospect. The product presentation should include FAB statements explaining how a product works and the benefits received. Focusing on your products USP should be addressed in this section.

Product
The physical item being offered for sale; although it can also include your services.

Prospect
A consumer before the sale is made, a prospective customer.

Rapport
A connection or harmonious relationship.

Referral
A recommendation or personal introduction made by your customer or prospect. Referrals can often be the strongest leads you can work with. A referral usually indicates a god relationship with your customer.

Second level questions
Additional questions that are generated by your prospects answers to your initial questions, these are usually more in-depth and specific than the initial questions.

Self-motivation
Having the initiative to engage in an activity without the supervision or motivation of another.

Self-realization
The understanding of ones situation and future potential.

Steps of the sale
The steps of the sale are the essential building blocks or sequence of events from the initial contact with the prospect through to the close of the sale and ending with your follow up. The steps of the sale, as presented in this book are:

1.   Greeting
2.   Establishing credibility
3.   Discovery
4.   Product presentation
5.   Creating urgency
6.   Closing the sale
7.   Addressing objections
8.   Follow-up

Sticker Shock
Your prospects reaction or shock to the price you ask if you have not justified your asking price sufficiently in the prospects mind. Recall the example of the MARCO1606 diving helmet.

Third-party story
Use real or fictional characters that are similar to your prospect. This third-party customer will have had a similar problem or concern your prospect currently has. Show or explain how this customer solved their problem. An example of a great third party story is the story of Dan the carpet kicker; this story was very effective in overcoming the 'I need to think about it' objection. Third party stories can have a happy or sad ending depending on whether or not the prospect you are using in the story purchased.

Trial close

An effective sales technique that sees the salesperson testing their prospect's readiness to purchase by asking 'opinion' type questions to elicit how the prospect feels about what has been said or shown. Trial closes usually follow positive buying signals. See Closing questions.

Uniqueness

A feature that is unique to your product that your competition can not offer.

Up-sell

Every time you sell an item, sell another item with it. The best example of this is in shoe sales, every time you purchase pair of shoes, you are most likely asked if your would like either leather protector, extra shoe laces or a new pair of socks. Up-selling is often easy as your customer has already agreed to the most expensive aspect of their purchase.

USP

USP is an acronym for Unique Selling Point or Proposition. The unique features or benefits that only your product can offer the prospect making your product competitively strong.

WIIFM

This is an acronym for 'what's in it for me?' This is a primary question that may or may not be expressed by your prospects. Keep WIIFM in the back of your mind every time you mention a feature and its benefit.

About the Author

In his first year in retail sales in the hot tub / pool industry, he generated almost $2,000,000 in sales. Marco Longley is a been-there, done-that sales professional that has seen every side of sales, from working in retail up to and including holding senior sales management positions with several major hot tub manufacturers. He has worked with sales professionals from Canada to Europe and has enjoyed time spent teaching and working with sales teams in the Caribbean and Mexico.

Marco's sales seminars and sales training book examine the numerous and crucial steps required to close the sale. With over three decades of sales experience, he has walked the walk and now shares his experiences and insights that have resulted in continuous record-breaking sales figures.

With an innate understanding of human nature, and by focusing on how to better understand customers' needs, Marco lays out a detailed road map of the sales process and what goes on in the mind of the customer to motivate their purchase. His seminars and training guides provide an in-depth, step-by-step method of how to work with and for your prospects, from the minute they walk into your store through to the purchase of your product and become customers.

Aside from being a professional salesman, Marco is happiest in front of an audience. In addition to be an author and sales trainer, he is also an award-winning inventor, a highly accredited scuba diving instructor and a professional magician.

He lives in Langley, British Columbia, with his soulmate and wife, Anne; two cats, Felix and Fabio; and a super dog named Roxy.